On Your Bike
Cambridgeshire

Other areas covered in our *On Your Bike* series include:

Bristol & Bath

Cheshire

The Chilterns

The Cotswolds

Derbyshire & Nottinghamshire

Devon

Essex

Hertfordshire & Rutland

Lancashire

Leicestershire & Rutland

Lincolnshire

Norfolk & Suffolk

Somerset

Surrey

Sussex

Thamesside

On Your Bike
Cambridgeshire

Sue and Paul Thomas

COUNTRYSIDE BOOKS
NEWBURY, BERKSHIRE

COUNTRYSIDE BOOKS
3 Catherine Road
Newbury, Berkshire

To view our complete range of books,
please visit us at
www.countrysidebooks.co.uk

ISBN 1 85306 890 X

Photographs by the authors
Cover picture supplied by Cyclographic Publications

Designed by Graham Whiteman
Produced through MRM Associates Ltd., Reading
Printed in Italy

CONTENTS

AREA MAP SHOWING THE LOCATIONS OF THE RIDES

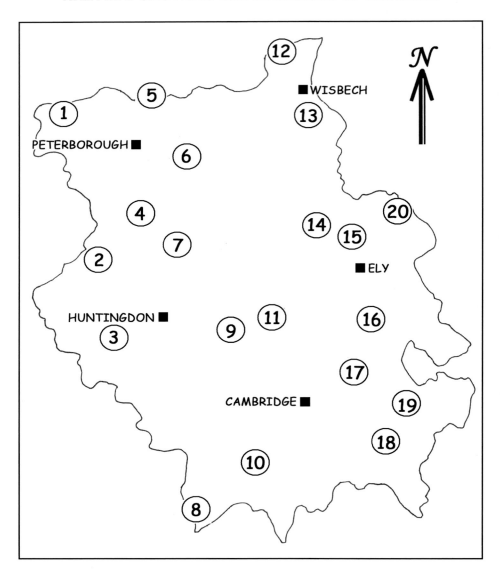

INTRODUCTION

T he county of Cambridgeshire, incorporating the old county of Huntingdonshire, is at the centre of the shires, bordering Lincolnshire and Norfolk in the north, Suffolk to the east, Essex and Hertfordshire to the south, and Bedfordshire and Northamptonshire to the west. It comprises a mixture of fenland and rolling hills, with agriculture dominating beyond the confines of the main cities, most notably Peterborough and Cambridge itself.

The Fens, in particular, offer a great environment for cycling, with few hills and little traffic, and everywhere there is evidence of the ongoing battle to drain the land, a campaign that has been underway since at least Roman times. Our rides range from the ancient landscape of the silt fen around The Wash to the more modern landscape of the inland peat fen with its dramatic shrinkage, as seen at Holme Fen, now the lowest place in Britain at around 10 ft below sea level.

Away from the flatlands of the Fens the surrounding hills can be surprisingly demanding, or perhaps it is just the contrast! Nevertheless they make for equally interesting cycling with their fair share of attractions and distractions along the way – from the partly natural at Grafham Water to the very man-made at the Imperial War Museum in Duxford.

Even in the major cities of Cambridgeshire, cyclists are increasingly offered safe and pleasant alternatives to traffic-choked roads, and Peterborough is arguably one of the best examples in the whole of the UK. The 'Green Wheel' circles the city, with spokes giving easy access to the centre itself. Segments of the Wheel feature in several of our rides – a particular highlight being the Millennium Bridge over the River Nene.

Perhaps the one unifying theme of the varying aspects of the Cambridgeshire landscape is water. Even away from the wetlands of the Fens, it is much in evidence, with lakes and major rivers draining through the area, and all that water means an abundance of wildlife, particularly birdlife. These rides offer the solitude to enjoy this in one of England's least populous counties.

Sue and Paul Thomas

GUIDE TO USING THIS BOOK

Each route is preceded by information to help you:

There are 20 **circular routes** of varying length, from 12½ to 27 miles, aimed at the family and leisure cyclist, rather than the hardened enthusiast, and including rides ideal for the complete novice. However, many of the routes are close enough together to allow them to be linked to provide longer runs for the more ambitious and give a good introduction to experienced cyclists new to the area.

The **route descriptions** with respect to difficulty are to some extent subjective and dependent on how you approach the ride. For example a 5-mile, off-road route is easy if taken slowly – walking up hills and avoiding obstacles – but tackle it at cross-country competition pace and it will be hard. Remember too, especially in the Fens, headwinds can make even the easiest route a serious challenge. The descriptions have been made as brief as possible, while still being readable. The intention is that you should be able to read and hold the relevant fragment in your mind between landmarks.

All routes start at a point where **parking** is available and, where possible, near a **rail station**. Where a station is not close to the

described starting point, one is usually nearby at some point en route, and this is highlighted in the description. Rail operators normally allow bikes to be carried free of charge, though sometimes pre-booking is required and the carriage of tandems, trikes and other larger cycles may be restricted. Regulations do vary, so call and check with the station before setting out.

Sketch maps are included, together with full route descriptions. While it should be possible to follow the routes using just this guide, it is recommended that you also carry a more detailed map (see Equipment and Safety over page). This will add to your enjoyment, and help should you stray from the route. The sketch maps are not to scale, and their own scale varies, with complicated areas requiring more detail than straightforward sections. To aid usability, only information that helps in following the route is included. Specifically, types of road junction – roundabout, mini roundabout, traffic lights and so on – are not differentiated, being simply shown as a junction; the accompanying text will add further detail. In built-up areas minor junctions are not shown.

Distances are 'map-measured' and the actual distance you travel will be slightly more where hills and

diversions are taken.
Brief details of pubs and teashops are included so that you can obtain **refreshment** en route.

Each ride description ends with details of the major **'sights and sounds'** you will encounter. There is so much to do and see in this area that not everything can be included here, and other notable attractions may be mentioned in the route introduction; others are left for you to discover.

Remember, things can change, pubs close, off-road tracks deteriorate – others are repaired. So be prepared – while every care has been taken to ensure accuracy, things may not be quite as advertised!

WHEN TO GO
Cambridgeshire has something to offer in all seasons, and everyone will have their own favourites. Ours are spring and autumn with their more dramatic light and variety of foliage, plus the added bonus of fewer crowds at popular locations. However, being largely agricultural, minor roads can be muddy during autumn when root crops are being lifted. And in all seasons it is best to avoid the Fens on very windy days.

The routes in this guide generally avoid off-road tracks that are poor during the winter months, and so are suitable all year round. If you are planning to explore other bridleways, bear in mind that they can be very muddy in winter and become overgrown in summer, often being at their best in the autumn and early spring.

Remember that cycling off-road on footpaths is not permitted. If you do explore, keep to bridleways, byways and RUPPs (Roads Used as Public Paths), or other routes where cycling is clearly indicated as being allowed.

In terms of the best time of day, and day of the week, this varies according to the route. Weekends are a popular time near tourist attractions, which means more traffic on country roads nearby, especially on summer Sundays. As anywhere, Saturdays are shopping days, and the roads around towns are busy from late morning to late afternoon.

Outside the rush hours (especially the 'school run') the roads away from the A roads and main towns are much quieter during the week. However, especially during winter, attractions may be closed, or have restricted opening. Also at busy times of the agricultural year country roads can be busy with heavy machinery, though tractor drivers do generally seem to be more considerate than car drivers.

EQUIPMENT AND SAFETY
Ordnance Survey 1:50,000 **Landranger maps** are the best for cycling, and these are the ones recommended and detailed in each chapter.

Nearer to large centres of

population you will come across **traffic** even on quiet lanes, and occasionally the routes in this guide by necessity follow or cross busier roads – though these are avoided wherever possible. It is important that you know how to cycle in traffic. Remember, ride confidently and, if necessary, walk your bike on the pavement. Any potentially busy roads and crossings are highlighted in the text; please take extra care at these points.

The routes in this book are mostly on roads, though there are some off-road sections, and some of the less-used lanes can be potholed and gravel strewn. The **type of bike** to use is a matter for personal preference, but, in our opinion, for general leisure-use a mountain bike or its less chunky cousin the hybrid offer best value for money and optimum comfort.

Make sure your bike is well maintained and safe – it is easier than trying to put something right when you are miles from anywhere. There are, however, **repairs** you need to be prepared for, the main one being a puncture. The chance of a puncture can be reduced by ensuring that tyres are not under inflated, but especially off road you will eventually succumb. So, carry a spare tube, tyre levers and a small pump, it is also worth taking instant repair patches in case you have more than one puncture to deal with.

After punctures, the most common problems relate to things coming loose, the chain breaking, frayed cables snapping, or spokes breaking, good maintenance will prevent all. These things are not frequent occurrences, so don't be put off, but for peace of mind you may want to look at the various multi-tools on the market. These are very compact and light, and can handle most emergency jobs.

A **bicycle maintenance book** (Haynes do a very good one) will explain how to effect repairs and show you how to do at least the more simple maintenance jobs on your bike and will quickly pay for itself.

There are various **bag and pannier systems** available to carry your tools and spares, together with food, a camera, spare clothing etc. This is easier and less restrictive than using a rucksack, though this is very much a matter of personal choice. Bottle cages will carry your water bottles – remember to take enough and refill as required; on a hot summer's day dehydration can start surprisingly quickly.

Clothing needs to be non-restrictive and comfortable, and there should be nothing loose to become entangled with moving bicycle parts. There are two pieces of specialist gear you may want to consider from the outset. Firstly, padded cycling shorts – they can make a great difference to your comfort on a day in the saddle. Secondly, waterproofs – good, breathable, waterproofs are a must unless you are sure of fine weather. As for cycling jackets, specific versions are cut to cover the lower back without getting in the way when dismounting, but any breathable fabric jacket will suffice.

A cycling helmet is recommended. There is much debate around this subject and helmet use is not compulsory, but there is evidence that helmets do reduce the severity of injuries sustained and save lives. We always wear ours.

FURTHER INFORMATION

If you get more involved, you will probably want to keep up to date with what is happening locally and nationally on the cycling scene. The popular press is dominated by mountain bike magazines, but more all-round titles are published and there is also a wealth of information available on the web.

The National Cycling Network has been big news in recent years, and Sustrans – the sustainable transport charity driving this – are active locally as well as nationally. Their website and newsletters provide an overview and updates on the network, and maps and books cover the detail. The major routes passing through Cambridgeshire areas are 11, 51 and 63.

There are many other cycle rides described for this area and local Tourist Information Centres will have details, maps and guides. Nationally, the Cycle Touring Club (CTC) is the largest cycling organisation and local groups in the area organise rides and social events.

Contact details
Sustrans: PO Box 21,
Bristol, BS99 2HA
www.sustrans.org.uk

CTC: Cotterell House, 69 Meadrow,
Godalming, Surrey GU7 3HS
www.ctc.org.uk

1

Hills and Holes and the Green Wheel North-West

16 or 22 miles

Peterborough is extremely well served by cycling routes, and the Green Wheel is one of the highlights. Surrounding the city with 'spokes' allowing easy access to and from the centre, it features in several of the rides in this book. This route starts from Barnack, the source of much local building stone over the centuries, and passes through villages rich with pretty stone, thatch and Collyweston slated cottages. There is a recommended diversion to visit another of Peterborough's great cycling and general recreational facilities, Ferry Meadows, with its cycle trails, lakes and steam railway.

Map: OS Landranger 142 Peterborough (GR 073049).

Starting point: Barnack, which is on the B1443 south-east of Stamford. The route starts from the parking marked on the OS map on the Barnack to Wittering road; it is on the left just before the end of the speed restriction on leaving the village. There is also parking by the Hills and Holes on the Southorpe road.

By train: Peterborough, from where the route can be joined in Ferry Meadows in approximately 4 miles via good cycleway.

Refreshments: This route is extremely well served by excellent old pubs and inns – but try not to stop at them all! In Barnack there is the Millstone, very welcoming, with good food and a family room. In Castor choose between the Prince of Wales Feathers, the Royal Oak and Fratelli's, a highly recommended Italian restaurant in the old Fitzwilliam Arms – all of which are full of character and welcome families. Another Fitzwilliam Arms in Marholm is open all day Monday to Saturday, and is an attractive thatched pub with a reputation for good food, and finally, also known for its food, there is Ye Olde White Hart in Ufford.

The route: This is a rolling route, with a couple of moderate climbs out of the Nene Valley and back onto the limestone hills above. The roads used are not busy, but you will encounter some traffic, particularly between Marholm and Barnack, and also through Castor, so care is required here and also at the roundabout with the A47, but all in all, this is an ideal family route.

Ye Olde White Hart at Ufford

From the Wittering road head back towards Barnack and at the junction **turn R**, signed for Southorpe and Ufford. Pass a left turn, which leads to the Millstone public house, and then on the right the Hills and Holes with layby parking and information boards.

Leave the village, passing the gatehouse for Walcot Hall on the right, the walls of which are then followed for some way. After a sharp right bend, continue straight on where a left turn leads to Ufford. The road goes through Southorpe, a small hamlet with no facilities, and then bends and undulates for some way to a junction where **turn L**, signed for Upton and away from the A47. (Should you arrive at a junction with the busy A47 you missed the turn – so turn around.)

At the next junction **turn R**, again signed for Upton, with views to the right across the Nene valley. Keep right at the next junction, ignoring the 'no through road' into Upton, and descend towards the A47. At the roundabout with the A47 go straight across, signed for Ailsworth and Castor, taking **great care**.

At the junction with Main Street **turn R**, signed for Castor and Marholm. Now follow the traffic-calmed main route through the village, all the while heading for Marholm. Pass the Prince of Wales

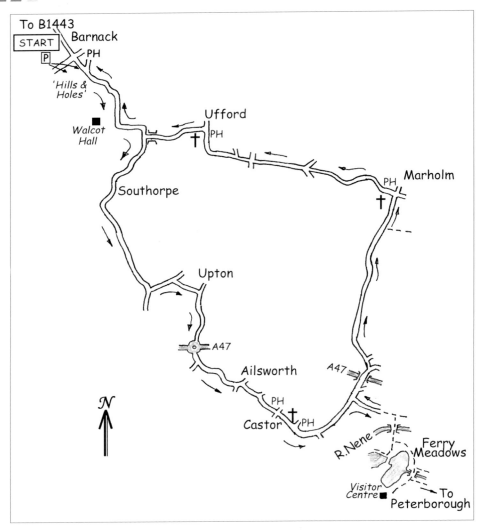

Feathers pub on the left, then the Fitzwilliam Arms Italian restaurant followed by the Royal Oak. Climb Love's Hill and out of Castor – note the cycle path on the left if required.

At the top of the hill, and just before crossing a bridge over the A47, a road to the right goes down to Ferry Meadows for a recommended diversion. Descend and at the end of the parking continue through the gate, passing a millennium milepost on the right with impressive views across the meadows. At the bottom of the hill **turn R** and cross the bridge over

Marholm village

the River Nene and at the next junction **turn L**, signed for National Cycle Network Route 63. Follow the path, keeping right and crossing a bridge to visit Ferry Meadows Visitor Centre, and explore further as you desire. Return then by the same route, and climb back to the junction at the top of Love's Hill, where **turn R**.

Now cross the bridge over the A47, heading for Marholm. Just after the bridge **turn L** on Marholm Road. Continue straight on where a branch of the Green Wheel goes to the right, heading for Bretton, to arrive in Marholm after just over 2 miles, passing the impressive-looking church on the left.

At the T-junction **turn L**, heading for Ufford, passing the Fitzwilliam Arms on the right. Leave Marholm now on a busier road and after a series of Z-bends continue straight on at the junction where minor roads go left and right, and straight on again at the next junction, all the while heading for Ufford.

In Ufford **turn L** by the White Hart with the church on your left. Leave Ufford and cross a bridge to a T-junction where **turn R** to return to Barnack on the route used on the outward journey.

The Millennium Milepost and Ferry Meadows

BARNACK

This village is built on land from which ragstone was quarried from Roman times up to the 16th century, some being used in the construction of nationally important buildings such as Crowland Abbey and the cathedrals at Peterborough and Ely. In 1976 a National Nature Reserve was created on the 22 hectares of the old quarry workings. These spoil tips, now known as the **HILLS AND HOLES**, support a variety of beautiful and rare wild plants and grasses.

FERRY MEADOWS COUNTRY PARK

The 500 acres of cycle and walking trails, together with lakes, rivers, a nature reserve and a steam railway, provide a welcome oasis in the suburbs of a large city. There is a cafeteria, bar and picnic area; and water sports and cycle hire are available.

NENE VALLEY RAILWAY

The steam and diesel locomotives on this 7½ mile standard gauge line are guaranteed to transport you back to the golden age of the railways. Running from Peterborough to Wansford via Ferry Meadows, the line also caters for special events such as weddings, birthdays, Drive a Locomotive and Santa's Special. Details are available on a talking timetable: 01780 784404.

The Nene-Ouse Watershed and the Northamptonshire Border

18 miles

This ride is a tour of the hilly area between the valleys of the rivers Nene and Great Ouse that also sits astride the border between Cambridgeshire and Northamptonshire. The highest parts of this ridge, including the Thurning to Clopton road, also mark the watershed between the two rivers, with rain falling on the north-west of the road destined for the Nene, and that on the south-east for the Ouse, to be reunited some 60 miles or more later in The Wash.

Map: OS Landranger 142 Peterborough (GR 136801).

Starting point: Hamerton, reached from the A1(M) at Sawtry or Alconbury, or from the B660. There is parking at the zoo park if you intend to visit, otherwise there is roadside parking opposite and nearby, but please take care not to block access to tracks and farm gates.

By train: There is no suitable rail station for this route.

Refreshments: In Molesworth the Cross Keys public house is highly recommended, serving snacks, sandwiches and meals every lunchtime and evening. It has a pleasant outdoor seating area, a good range of beers and overnight accommodation. The only other pub on the route is the Swan in Old Weston, which also has an outdoor seating area. There is also a coffee shop and picnic area at Hamerton Zoo Park.

The route: A hilly ride, mostly on quiet roads, with just a couple of busy junctions. There is also one long section of off-road cycling, which follows a good bridleway that should be easily passable all year round.

From the zoo park, continue down the hill and into Hamerton. At a 'give way' **turn L** and then **almost immediately R** over the narrow bridge into the village. Keep with the road through a sharp right-hand bend by the church and continue to a T-junction at the end of Sawpit Lane, where **turn R**, then **L**, signed for Winwick.

The road undulates, climbing gradually, and in approximately 2 miles leads to a T-junction with the B660 in Winwick. **Turn L, then immediately R** on the minor road signed for Thurning.

The narrow bridge over the Alconbury Brook in Hamerton

Leave the village passing the Listers factory on the left and continue through several dips and climbs to arrive in Thurning and the T-junction by the church with its interesting tower. **Turn L**, signed for Clopton, and follow the pleasant road through open fields and by woodland to the village of Clopton and a junction where **turn L** on the B662. After a short way, and by the church, **turn R with care** on a minor road signed for Titchmarsh. At a sharp right bend, where the road goes right for Titchmarsh and Thrapston, continue straight ahead on the 'no through road'.

The rough tarmac road continues to a left bend by barns where keep with the road, ignoring a byway that goes straight ahead. At the end of the road, by the perimeter fence of RAF Molesworth, **turn R**, following the bridleway.

The bridleway initially follows broken tarmac to a gate, with the tarmac continuing to the fence; **turn R** here on the bridleway, which is now a grassy track. Note that the line of the bridleway is not immediately adjacent to the RAF base fence but just to the right, and to the right of the concrete post and wire fence.
The bridleway now follows the

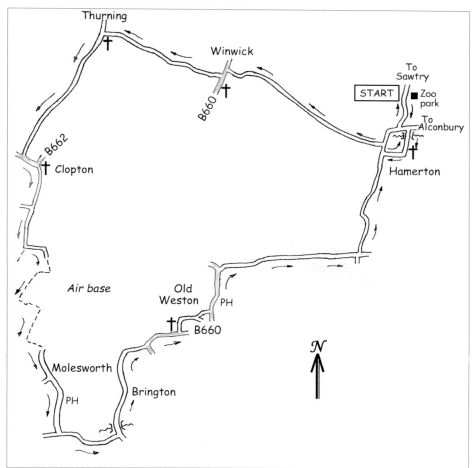

perimeter fence for some way, in summer the abundant wild flowers providing a contrast to the imposing sight of barbed wire and high fence. After tracking several bends in the fence the bridleway arrives at a small valley with a tarmac road by a closed gate into the air base.

Turn R on the tarmac road and follow the hill down into Molesworth, passing a junction

and the village noticeboard and phone box to the Cross Keys public house and on to a T-junction. **Turn L** here, signed for 'all other routes', and at the next 'give way' **turn L** for Brington. Cross the bridge and continue into the village.

After passing through the village, the road continues to climb to a sharp right bend, again approaching the perimeter of RAF

St Swithin's church, Old Weston

Molesworth. Pass the main entrance to the air base and keep with the road as it bends to the left and becomes the B660. Shortly, and just having passed the 'Old Weston' sign, **turn L** at a minor junction to pass by the church, St Swithin's, and on through the small village. Keep left at the first junction to arrive at a 'give way' where **turn L**, now back on the B road, passing the Swan public house on the right.

After leaving the village the road bends to the left at a minor junction where **turn R**, signed for Buckworth, Alconbury and the zoo park. This road continues on a more or less level course, following the line of an old Roman road to a

crossroads where **turn L**, signed for Hamerton, Sawtry and the zoo park. The minor road then twists and turns to Hamerton and the junction with Sawpit Lane visited earlier. **Turn R** here and retrace the outward journey to return to the parking and zoo park.

• •

HAMERTON ZOO PARK
Situated in 25 acres of parkland, Hamerton was opened as a conservation sanctuary in 1990, specialising in rare, endangered and unusual animals. A children's play area, coffee shop, gift shop and picnic areas are also available. Open every day except Christmas Day from 10.30 am to 6 pm in the summer, 10.30 am to 4 pm in the winter.

THURNING CHURCH
The walls of the church are made of coursed rubble with stone dressings, and the roofs are covered with lead. In the late 12th and early 13th centuries alterations and extensions took place, the details of which are not well documented – thought to be a consequence of employing a rather old mason! More alterations were made in the 15th century, including a new west wall, with a bell-turret and spirelet above. Further extensive alterations and restoration work took place in 1850, 1880 and again in 1902. Inside there are rows of box pews all labelled with the names of different farms.

RAF MOLESWORTH
Formerly part of a tri-base with Alconbury and Upwood, this is now largely unused since the USAF left in the 1990s.

3

The Grafham Water Cycle Track and Stow Longa

15½ miles

This route takes in most of the excellent 10 mile cycle track round Grafham Water and adds to it a diversion to the hills above and to the village of Stow Longa, making for a lengthier but more satisfying ride.

Map: OS Landranger 153 Bedford and Huntingdon (GR 164679).

Starting point: The Exhibition Centre on the north shore of Grafham Water, reached via the A1/B661 or from the A14 through Grafham. There is a charge for parking, but none for entering the reservoir site. A cycle hire centre and cycling shop are situated here.

By train: Huntingdon and St Neots stations are about equidistant from Grafham Water, but both would involve approximately an additional 6 miles each way and the use of busy roads, so this is not a recommended option.

Refreshments: There are few facilities on the route though the West Perry Visitor Centre has a very pleasant bar and restaurant overlooking the harbour with ample outdoor seating. It is open from 7 am until dusk seven days a week and sells tea, coffee, snacks, sandwiches and meals and also has a licensed bar. It is very family and cyclist friendly.

The route: The Grafham Water cycleway section of this route is excellent for new cyclists and children alike, being on a good surface and well signed throughout. However, care is required through West Perry where the route follows the main road. The diversion to Stow Longa involves a mixture of quiet lanes and bridleways with a couple of steep climbs.

From the car park join the waterside track and **turn R**. The track winds and undulates through woods before climbing a lane into Grafham, where **turn L**. Continue on the lane to a small parking area and then onto a track. Shortly at a junction **turn L** through a gate to keep with the cycle track, which then continues along the water's edge before climbing through woods and around a small inlet.

After the inlet and by a large pylon the cycle track continues round to the left but **turn R** on the track,

A cottage in Stow Longa

which is a bridleway across fields. At the top of the hill keep with the track to the right, passing the farm and then continuing on a concrete roadway to the public road where **turn R**. Cross a small valley and after going over a humpbacked bridge **turn L** on the second bridleway, which is also a farm track. Keep with the track as it curves to the right by the barns and before entering the derelict buildings. Stay on the good track as it bends left and then right before descending quite steeply into the valley below.

At the base of the descent the track bends right and then left through a field hedge and the bridleway then continues diagonally across the field ahead on what can be a bumpy surface broken up by horses. This is a short section and quickly leads to a track where **turn R**, heading for the spire of Spaldwick church.

At a junction with a byway **turn L**, and then where the byway track turns right, continue straight across the field on a bridleway to emerge by the buildings and join the road. Turn right to visit Spaldwick, or **turn L** to continue the route and climb gradually to Stow Longa. In the village pass the intriguing village sign by the village green and Church Lane on the right leading to St Botolph's 13th-century church.

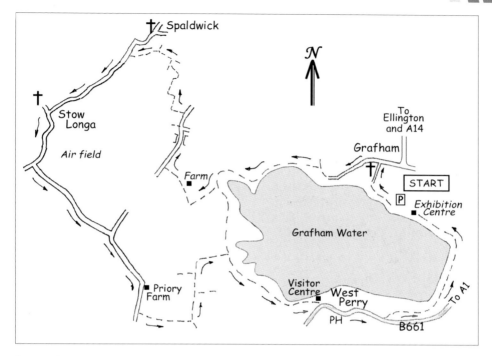

Leave Stow Longa, passing the old station master's cottage on the right, and then, shortly after passing the private airstrip and karting club on the left, **turn L**, signed for Easton and Stonely. Continue to a 'give way' in approximately 1 mile and **turn R**, signed for Stonely and Kimbolton. Ignore the first bridleway on the left just before Priory Farm, and after passing the farm **turn L** on the next bridleway through a small gated entrance. Initially a rough track along a field edge, the bridleway then leads to the edge of a wood and a junction with another bridleway where **turn L** on a good but rutted track.

At the next junction keep straight on where another good track descends to the right, then, where the good track bears left back towards Priory Farm, continue straight ahead on the now rough bridleway, still keeping with the wood edge. Pass an area of bird pens beyond which the bridleway becomes separated from the field by a thin hedge. At the end of the wood bear right with the bridleway and meet the Grafham Water cycleway by Littless Wood nature trail. **Turn R**.

The well-marked and good cycle track then leads to a car park for the West Perry Visitor Centre and the Harbour View restaurant and bar. Leave the car park and follow the cycle track, which is, in fact, the road through West Perry village, passing the pub on the right. On leaving the village and by Duberly Close join the cycle path on the left and **turn L** before the treatment works on the right, poorly signed as the cycle path.

The cycle track then leads more or less parallel with the road to the dam where the route proceeds below the dam wall to arrive back at the Exhibition Centre and car park.

Grafham Water

GRAFHAM WATER

This is one of a number of reservoirs managed by Anglian Water and open to the public, and its 10-mile lakeside circuit is popular with walkers, cyclists and joggers. A variety of bikes may be hired at the cycle hire centre; this could be a great opportunity to try out a tandem! As a Site of Special Scientific Interest the western side of the water has a large nature reserve with nature trails, information boards, a dragonfly pond and wildlife garden. There are also a number of bird hides situated around the lake from where the migrating flocks of waterfowl can be observed. Fishing, sailing, canoeing, water-skiing and windsurfing are also enjoyed and taught at Grafham Water. The Exhibition Centre houses displays showing the history of the reservoir and has a gift shop and café.

STOW LONGA

The church tower, at 200 ft, claims to be at the highest point in old Huntingdonshire. Also in the village is the intriguing village sign – clues to all of its contents can be found on the ride through the village. The church is obvious, and you will pass the old station master's cottage and the airfield as you leave the village; the fox is more of a mystery. One is clearly seen atop the thatch of the cottage opposite – maybe this used to be the village pub? Look carefully and you'll also see references to sheep, wildfowl and go-karts!

4

Holme Fen, Stilton and Glatton

18 miles

Starting out from the Holme Fen Nature Reserve, which is also home to the dramatic Fen Posts, shows just how much impact drainage has had on the land surface of the Fens. This ride visits settlements that grew up along the old Great North Road when journey times were measured in days not hours, including Stilton, an important stop in the days of coach travel, made famous by the cheese sold at the Bell Inn.

Map: OS Landranger 142 Peterborough (GR 203894).

Starting point: Holme Fen, reached via the B660 through Holme or from the A15 at Yaxley. There is parking by the nature reserve and Fen Posts.

By train: Peterborough station, from where the route could be joined in Yaxley, though this would add over 5 miles each way and make for a very long outing.

Refreshments: Stilton has several pubs and shops, including the famous Bell Inn, the original home of Stilton cheese. There are also pubs in Glatton (the Addison Arms, which has a beer garden) and near the end of the route in Holme. Sawtry has shops, public toilets and a number of pubs, including the Greystones which is open all day.

The route: A relatively long and quite hilly route along the fen edge. Although mostly following minor roads there are a couple of busy sections, including a short stretch of the A15. Dedicated cycleways do avoid many of the problems but, even so, coupled with the length, this makes the route unsuitable for a first outing, but should present no problems to those with a little experience.

From the parking by Holme Fen Nature Reserve head back towards Holme, over the level crossing and at the junction **turn R**, heading for Yaxley. The road leads to the fen edge and uplands at Yaxley, where **turn R** at the 'give way', then **turn L** on Church Street to climb, passing the impressive church on the left. Shortly **turn L** on Water Slade Road where Dovecote Lane goes to the right.

Keep **L** at the 'give way' where the road joins the A15. **Take care** as this is a busy road. Pass the Norman Cross Gallery on the right and continue into Norman Cross where leave the road and **turn L**

Bird hide in the nature reserve at Holme Fen

onto the cycleway and shared footpath signed for Stilton. The Norman Cross memorial is to the right across the A15.

The cycleway leads alongside the A1(M), and following a short climb comes to a small roundabout where **turn R** to cross the motorway by a bridge. At the next junction **turn L** and follow the road into Stilton. Just before the Bell Inn **turn R** by the phone box onto Church Street. Pass the church on the left and after a sharp right **turn L** onto Caldecote Road to climb out of the village. Continue straight ahead at a junction for Folksworth and descend into Caldecote, where keep

straight on, signed for The Giddings.

Climb again to a 'give way' where **turn L**, signed for Great Gidding. At the next junction **turn L** for Glatton and descend into the pretty village with its mix of thatched cottages and newer houses. Pass the church on the right and at the 'give way' **turn R** and **immediately** L onto Sawtry Road, soon passing the Addison Arms on the right.

The road winds and undulates into Sawtry where pass Church Street on the left then keep left at the green on Fen Lane. Note: A right turn by the green leads to the Greystones pub and shops. Fen Lane leads to a small roundabout where **turn L**, signed for the A1 South along with Connington, Stilton, Holme and Ramsey.

Cross the A1(M) by a bridge and at the next roundabout **turn L**. Note: There is a shared-use cycle path to the right if required. Pass St Andrew's cemetery on the right and then **turn R** on Cooks Lane to ride through farmland, now back onto the low-lying peat fen. Keep left with the rough road where straight on is a 'no through road' and at a further junction **turn R** and **shortly L**, signed for Holme. At a junction in front of the small business airport **turn R**, passing the airport buildings on the left. Ignore a right turn for Coddington Fen and at the 'give way' **turn R with**

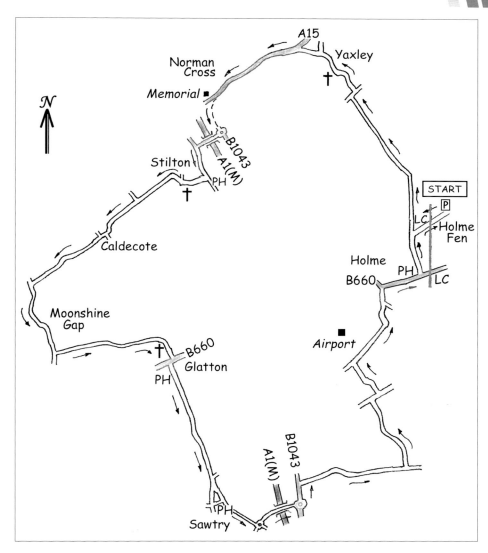

care then just before the level crossing, and by the Admiral Wells pub, **turn L**, signed for Yaxley.

In approximately ½ mile **turn R**, signed for Holme Fen Posts, to return to the start point and the parking.

HOLME FEN POSTS

The posts provide a visual record of the extent of peat shrinkage that occurred after draining Whittlesey Mere in 1851. As a result of this it is now one of the lowest places in England at around 10 ft below sea level.

The Bell at Stilton

HOLME FEN NATURE RESERVE

The path opposite the posts leads into the nature reserve and to a bird hide with extensive views over the mere. It is now managed by English Nature who are dedicated to ensuring the survival of the rare plants and animals that live on the fen.

NORMAN CROSS

The memorial, a bronze eagle on a column, was erected in memory of the many French prisoners of war who died here during the Napoleonic Wars. At that time the Fens were an important waterway, the prisoners being landed in flat-bottomed boats at Yaxley.

STILTON

Once an important stagecoach stop on the Great North Road, this was where travellers purchased the famous Stilton cheese (though it was actually produced near Melton Mowbray). The village hosts an annual 'cheese rolling' contest when teams from surrounding villages bowl a 'cheese' (a painted log) down the High Street. The prize is a crate of beer and, of course – a whole Stilton. Local charities benefit from the event.

Crowland Abbey and the Green Wheel North-East

13½ miles

Another flirt with Peterborough's Green Wheel, this time combining parts of the North-Eastern section with delightful waterside riding along the River Welland, plus a visit to historic Crowland with its abbey and 14th-century, three-arched, bridge.

Map: OS Landranger 142 Peterborough (GR 235106).

Starting point: Just outside Crowland on the B1166 heading for Market Deeping, where parking is available on the roadside by the picnic area and lake. Crowland is situated just west of the A1073 between Spalding and Eye.

By train: From Peterborough the route can be joined at Peakirk via the Green Wheel, though this would add approximately 6 miles each way.

Refreshments: The Bridge Inn Restaurant and Freehouse is near the starting point and serves good food at lunchtime and in the evening on Monday to Thursday, and all day on Friday, Saturday and Sunday. There are several pubs and shops in the Deepings and Crowland, and also a pub in Peakirk.

The route: A short, level route on minor roads and off-road track, with plenty of diversions to maintain interest along the way. Being close to Peterborough the roads do carry more traffic than in the more remote areas of the Fens, but they are still relatively quiet, though, as ever, care is required, especially in Crowland.

Continue on the B1166 by the lake, heading towards Market Deeping, and cross over the river, with the water tower and Bridge Inn ahead. **Turn L** at the junction and follow the road along the bank of the River Welland towards Market Deeping, a popular spot for fishermen and wildfowl alike.

Keep with the road as it drops away from the riverbank and shortly bends sharp right away from the river. Pass an exotic pet refuge on the left amongst the water-filled gravel pits to reach a small level crossing. Go over this and **turn L**, heading for Deeping St James, signed for Eastgate only. Follow the road as it winds into and through Deeping St James. Keep left with the road by the cross and church.

Crowland's magnificent abbey

After passing the post office, tearooms and Waterton Arms pub, **turn L** to cross the bridge back over this branch of the Welland, signed for the Green Wheel, Northborough and Peakirk. Note: Continuing straight on here leads to shops, pubs and a cycle repair shop should you need it.

Shortly after crossing the bridge **turn L** at a crossroads onto Peakirk Road. Continue, crossing the Maxey Cut which forms another branch of the Welland, and on into Peakirk. On the left are the buildings and lakes of the Peakirk Waterfowl Reserve, which closed in 2001. At the junction **turn L** back onto the Green Wheel, signed for Crowland; note that there is a pub just to the right at this junction.

Shortly go over a level crossing and join the cycle track on the left. Cross a bridge over another branch leading into the Welland and **turn L**, following the Green Wheel towards Crowland along the road into Sissons Farm Equestrian Centre. This now leads along the south bank of the Welland opposite the road followed earlier.

The track shortly branches away from the main river course to follow the edge of the wash, the flood defence between the river and the fen below. After approximately 2 miles, and having

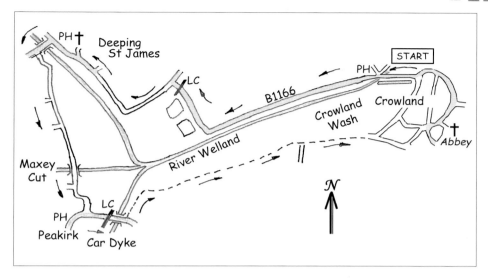

passed a number of owl boxes on the right, ignore a right turn on the Green Wheel and continue along the bank on National Cycle Network Route 63. Cross the border from Cambridgeshire back into Lincolnshire with Crowland Abbey in view in the distance.

On approaching Crowland keep with the bridleway on the high bank ignoring a minor tarmac road to the right, continuing to meet a road at a sharp bend on the edge of the village. **Turn L** here and then take the **first R** onto West Street to visit the abbey, Trinity Bridge and the shops and pubs of Crowland. After passing the bridge and shops, **turn R** onto the cobbled street by the library and sea and sand sculptures to visit the abbey. Return then by West Street to the same junction and **turn R** and then follow the road to the left to return to the parking.

THE DEEPINGS

This is the collective name for the villages of Market Deeping, Deeping St James, West Deeping and Deeping Gates, all of which border the banks of the River Welland and were part of the royal manor until they were sold in the 19th century. The name Deeping is thought to mean 'deep in the fen' or 'low-lying land'.

CROWLAND ABBEY

The abbey was established on the island of Croyland almost thirteen centuries ago by Guthlac, a soldier who became a monk. Originally a small church, it has now become one of the nation's most important Benedictine monasteries. The present church and ruins of the abbey are a magnificent sight and well worth a visit.

TRINITY BRIDGE

The bridge is composed of three arches, but is a one-arched structure, so may be said to represent the Divine 'Three in One' – hence its name. Although nowadays it is over dry land, when Crowland was a group of islands Trinity

Land, sea and sky sculpture at Crowland

Bridge was positioned at the point where the River Welland divided into two streams, one branch going past the abbey and being used for sanitation and sewerage, the other, main, branch continuing towards Spalding.

LAND, SEA AND SKY SCULPTURES

In front of Crowland Library, these unusual and colourful sculptures take the form of benches and were commissioned in 2002. They were inspired by the landscape and geography of the Fens but, as with anything different, when unveiled they did not prove popular with all the local people.

Whittlesey, Thorney and Flag Fen

16 miles

This route, rich in Fenland history, starts out from the small market town of Whittlesey and offers a fascinating diversion in the shape of the Flag Fen Bronze Age Centre and Museum, coupled with a visit to the magnificent Thorney Abbey. This ride also crosses the River Nene by Shanks Millennium Bridge, one of the highlights of the National Cycle Network in this area, and arguably the most impressive cycle bridge in the whole country.

Map: OS Landranger 142 Peterborough (GR 278962).

Starting point: Whittlesey station, where there is also parking for non-rail users. Alternatively, there is plenty of parking in the town centre itself. Whittlesey is on the A605 east of Peterborough.

By train: Whittlesey station, from where trains run to Peterborough, Ely, Thetford and Norwich.

Refreshments: Whittlesey has many shops, pubs and restaurants. On the route there is a café in the Flag Fen Visitor Centre, and in Thorney the Rose and Crown has an outdoor seating area and serves food. Just before returning to Whittlesey there is also the Dog-in-a-Doublet public house on the banks of the Nene by the sluice gate.

The route: This ride follows mostly off-road cycle facilities and quiet byways, but the B1040 from Thorney to Whittlesey can be quite busy, especially the final section from the Dog-in-a-Doublet and particularly at commuter times when it is used as a rat-run into Peterborough. This makes the full ride unsuitable for groups with smaller children – however, an out-and-back run along the off-road section from Whittlesey to Flag Fen would make an ideal introductory ride for all ages.

From the station **turn R** heading into Whittlesey, following the pedestrian and cycleway signs and passing the Railway pub on the right. At the first major junction continue straight on, signed for the town centre only and National Cycle Network Route 63, which you will follow all the way to Shanks Millennium Bridge.

At the next junction use the cycle lane at the 'give way' and cross onto the High Causeway pedestrian

The Iron Age roundhouse at Flag Fen

zone. At the end of the pedestrian zone, dismount and cross via the pedestrian crossing then continue straight ahead on High Causeway.

Turn L by the thatched New Crown pub and then cross the B road via the cycle crossing next to a millennium milepost. Continue along Gracious Street and then **turn R** at the junction, still signed for Route 63. At the next junction **turn L** onto a more major road, and continue to a point where the road bends sharply to the left. Continue straight ahead here on Route 63, now following a rough track signed for the Peterborough Millennium Green Wheel. The track shortly turns to the right,

and then bends to the left with the tall chimneys of the brickworks coming into view. Pass another millennium milepost, as the views into the brickworks and quarry open up on the left. After a slightly wooded area at a junction keep to the right on Route 63 where a left turn follows an alternative branch of the Green Wheel on Local Route 21. Note: Just along Route 21 there is an information board about the Green Wheel generally and Whittlesey Island.

The track then leads to the impressive Shanks Millennium Bridge where you cross the River Nene and **turn L** on the cycleway. After a short way, and by a small

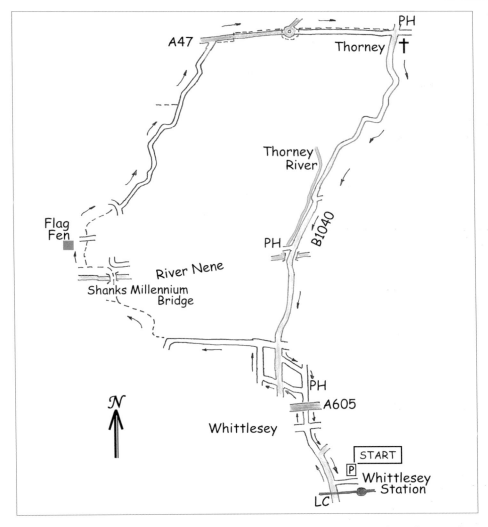

pumping station, **turn R** on Route 21, now leaving Route 63 and the Nene embankment. The cycle path leads past the Flag Fen Visitor Centre, crossing the access road just after a small bridge and information boards. Look out for hidden sculptures along the side of the track.

Where the track reaches the road keep with the cycleway, crossing **with care** onto Willow Hall Way, heading for Eye. Follow this quiet road, ignoring a left turn for the cycle route towards Eye, and in approximately 3 miles reach a junction with the busy A47. **Do not** join the road, but immediately

The National Cycle Network crosses the Nene via Shanks Millennium Bridge

before the junction take the cycle path on the right, running alongside the A47.

In approximately 300 yards cross the A47 on the cycle path **with care** to now take the left-hand side of the carriageway. On approaching the new roundabout cross the road again to follow the cycleway around the south side of the roundabout and then re-cross the old A47 to rejoin the cycleway on the north side of the road leading into the village. Note: At the time of writing the bypass and new roundabout are under construction and details of the planned cycle route described above are based on information from the council. These may vary once constructed, but the route should be well signed.

Continue now into Thorney, taking care when crossing entrances and in places where the surface is poor. Pass a windmill on the left and views of the abbey to the right to reach a junction by the Rose and Crown, where either rejoin the road or dismount and cross by the pedestrian crossing to **turn R** on the B1040.

Pass the abbey and keep with the B road as it winds away from Thorney, **taking care** on the bends.

The road then continues alongside the Thorney River, crossing the River Nene and back into Cambridgeshire by the Dog-in-a-Doublet pub after approximately 3 miles. The road now becomes busier and leads into Whittlesey across wash-lands that are often flooded in the winter. At the traffic lights make use of the cyclists' advance start lane if desired to continue straight ahead and then by the Ram Inn, **fork L.**

Follow the road round to the right to rejoin the outward route by the thatched New Crown. Cross the road back to the pedestrian zone and return to the station by the same route followed earlier.

● ●

WHITTLESEY ISLAND

This was once an isolated piece of high ground in the fens linked to the nearby Northy Island by a fen causeway, which runs through Flag Fen visited on the route.

WHITTLESEY TOWN

A rich variety of buildings can be seen, with some particularly interesting thatched cottages on Gracious Street. The town is still known for its traditional Straw Bear Festival, held on the Saturday nearest to Plough Monday, where a man dressed as a straw bear collects money for charity whilst dancing around the streets accompanied by Morris Dancers.

BRITAIN'S BRONZE AGE CENTRE, FLAG FEN

This continuing research project, which constantly unearths new finds of late-Bronze Age artefacts, is open throughout the year. The site was discovered as a result of survey work undertaken in 1982 on the newly cleaned dyke sides. Numerous finds of wood, leather and plant material were made as a result of the anaerobic environment in which they were preserved. Highlights of the centre include the remains of a 3,000 year old line of posts, which formed a fen causeway, housed in an undercover display hall, and the 20-acre park with reconstructed Iron Age and Bronze Age buildings. The centre also houses the FLAG FEN HERITAGE VISITOR CENTRE, which was constructed as part of the Millennium Green Wheel Project with funding from Peterborough Environment City Trust and the Millennium Commission. It is open daily except between 24th December and 2nd January and has a gift shop, toilets and tearoom, along with a wonderful museum housing weapons, jewelry and sacrificial items unearthed at the site.

SHANKS MILLENNIUM BRIDGE

Carries National Cycle Network route 63 over the River Nene and links the northern and southern parts of Peterborough's Green Wheel. It was built using recycled steel collected at the city's recycling plant.

THORNEY ABBEY

Thorney, too, was an island in the Fens and was used as a monastic settlement as far back as the 7th century. The original monastery was destroyed in AD 870 and parts of the Norman rebuild are incorporated in the current abbey.

Ramsey, Warboys and the Fen Edge

17½ miles

Winding, hilly lanes and flat fenland droves combine to offer a great variety of cycling on this ride around a relatively populous area of the Fens. The route starts out on the higher ground in Upwood, first passing through Warboys before sweeping down to the fen below for a brief period of solitude, followed by a visit to the busy and historic market town of Ramsey.

Map: OS Landranger 142 Peterborough (GR 260825).

Starting point: Upwood, which is situated south-west of Ramsey. There is space for parking on the road in the village near the church and pub.

By train: There is no suitable rail station for this route.

Refreshments: There are shops, pubs and restaurants in Warboys and Ramsey, plus quieter pubs in the villages of Upwood and Wistow.

The route: Some reasonably busy roads are used. Also Warboys and particularly Ramsey are popular places, so competence when cycling in traffic is required.

Follow the High Street in Upwood to the south, and at its end **turn L** onto Meadow Road, then at the junction with the busier road **turn R**, signed for Little Raveley and Huntingdon. In Great Raveley pass the right turn for Wood Walton, climb slightly and take the **next L turn**, signed for Wistow. A quieter road now zigzags across the hilltop before crossing a small valley to a junction where **turn L** again, signed for Wistow. Continue through the village, passing the Three Horseshoes and the church, and shortly afterwards by the telephone box **turn R**, signed for Warboys and Ramsey, on Bridge Street.

Continue to a junction with the busier B1040 and **turn R with care**, signed for Warboys, which is reached in approximately 1 mile. Continue to a junction by the clocktower and **turn L**, signed for parking and the village centre. Pass pubs and shops, keeping left at the next junction by the duck pond and then **turn L** at the T-junction by the Royal Oak.

At the next junction on a bend **turn L** onto Station Road and leave

Ramsey Abbey gatehouse

the village on the more minor road. Keep left at a fork, passing the entrance to a landfill site on the left, and continue on the straight road across the fen for approximately 3 miles.

At a staggered junction by a garage marked as the White Swan, **turn L**. After a straight section the road winds through a group of farm buildings and crosses over the Ash Drain to a junction where **turn L**, signed for Ramsey, on Ramsey Hall Drove. The road now winds and climbs slightly away from the fen and on into Ramsey by the church and ruins of the abbey on the right.

At the 'give way' in Ramsey **turn L** and pass through the town centre with its shops, pubs and restaurants, taking care around parked cars and traffic. On leaving the town, and where the B1040 bends to the left by the White Lion, **turn R with care**. Follow the more minor road to climb again, passing the RAF camp on the right, to arrive back in Upwood, where take the **second R** by the Upwood village sign, signed for Upwood, to arrive back at the T-junction in the village by the church and pub.

● ●

WARBOYS

This typical fenland village has a rather unusual claim to fame – the execution of three witches in 1593. They were convicted of bewitching 14 people, though as with many similar cases in the past the charge was later thought to have been made up.

RAMSEY ABBEY GATEHOUSE

Now in the hands of the National Trust, this richly-carved gatehouse has an

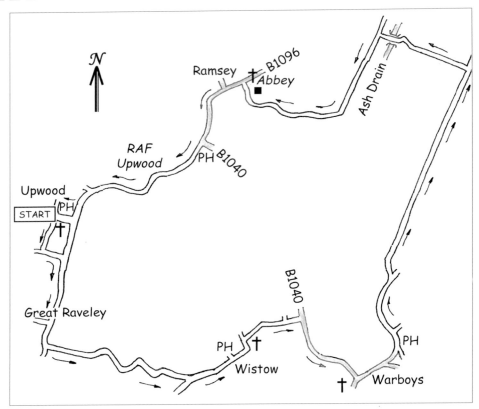

ornate oriel window and was built in the late 15th century. It forms part of the remains of a Benedictine abbey, which, like the abbeys of Thorney and Crowland visited on other routes, was built on an island in the Fens. It is open for viewing from 1st April until 31st October, seven days a week, between the hours of 10 am and 5 pm. There is no admission charge.

RAMSEY

Once an island in the Fens, Ramsey became a thriving port when joined to the inland waterway of the River Nene. The railways followed in the 19th century, with two separate lines built by rival companies. Both have since closed. In 1975 the centre of the town was designated a conservation area as it is in the enviable position of having several buildings of special historical or architectural interest.

RAF UPWOOD

Accommodation and medical facilities for Air Force personnel stationed at the nearby bases of Alconbury and Molesworth were provided here. After the USAF moved out in the 1990s the site was purchased by a property developer, but still remains undeveloped.

8

Three Counties' Borders around the Source of the River Rhee

20 miles

The counties of Bedfordshire, Hertfordshire and Cambridgeshire meet at a point in open country between Dunton and Guilden Morden, and this ride makes a circuit along winding roads through rolling countryside roughly centred on that point. There are few major tourist attractions on this route, which means less traffic and more time to appreciate the natural and man-made landscape traversed.

Map: OS Landranger 153 Bedford and Huntingdon (GR 285427).

Starting point: Steeple Morden, where there is plenty of parking by the recreation ground and just beyond the village hall. If approaching from the A505 to the south, turn left just after the church.

By train: Ashwell station, from where the route can be joined either in Ashwell or Steeple Morden, in approximately 1¼ or 2¼ miles respectively.

Refreshments: The obvious half-time pub stop is the Chequers, just off the route in Wrestlingworth. It serves snacks and meals at lunchtimes and in the evenings and has an outdoor play area and beer garden. There are also pubs in many of the other villages visited, though note that the March Hare in Dunton is not always open at lunchtime. Ashwell is a large and well equipped village with various facilities. There is also the Waggon and Horses close to the start point in Steeple Morden. This is a pleasant and welcoming village pub with outdoor seating and food available.

The route: A relatively long ride, with noticeable ups and downs. It mainly follows minor roads, though some moderate traffic will be encountered, particularly close to the larger villages.

Follow the track by the village hall back to the road and **turn R** and **shortly L** before reaching the pub, signed for Litlington. After the post office and village sign, descend to a Z-bend and then climb out of the village. The road then levels and descends gently with good views to the left and right into Litlington. Immediately on entering the village, with the church on the right, **turn L** onto Church Street,

The dilapidated windmill on the approach to Steeple Morden

heading for Abington Pigotts.

The rolling minor road leads into Abington Pigotts by woodland, then through a sharp right bend into the village by the Pig and Abbot public house. Continue, passing Church Lane on the left, and leave the village with the duck pond on the left.

The single-track road then winds to a T-junction by a barn. **Turn L** here and proceed between open fields into Shingay and a series of bends, which lead to a T-junction where **turn L**. Follow the busier road to Guilden Morden and at the junction **turn R**, heading for

Wrestlingworth on Fox Hill Road. Keep straight on at the next junction and, after leaving the village, follow the road as it passes an old windmill and riverside mill to the left, then crosses the River Cam (or Rhee) into Bedfordshire.

The road then climbs to a junction on the edge of Wrestlingworth where straight on leads to the pub. **Turn L** on the Eyeworth road. After a series of bends, climb into Eyeworth and on through this small village with no facilities, now heading for Dunton. **Take care** as although this is a minor road it does carry some traffic and is a bus route.

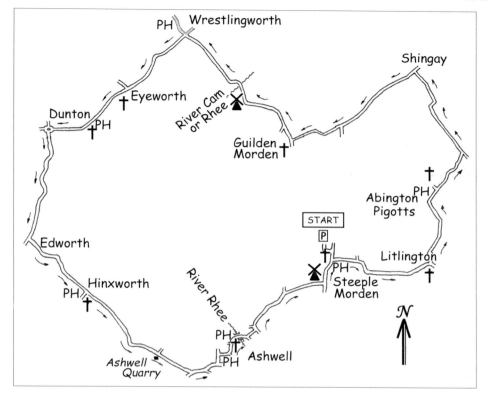

In Dunton keep with the road as it bends to the right by the March Hare pub and the post office, and then through a sharper right-hand bend out of the village to a small roundabout. **Turn L** here, heading for Edworth. The road winds between open fields and hedgerows to a minor junction on the edge of Edworth. **Turn L**, signed for Edworth, Hinxworth and Ashwell. This more minor road quickly leads through the small hamlet of Edworth and on to Hinxworth, crossing the county boundary into Hertfordshire. Pass the Three Horseshoes pub and continue straight on through the village.

A very pleasant road by an avenue of trees leads to a sharp bend then passes Loves Lane and Ashwell Quarry Nature Reserve on the right. At the 'give way' **turn L**, continue into the village and, just before the Rose and Crown pub, **turn L** by the village store onto Gardiners Lane. Almost immediately **turn R** onto Swan Street and with the village museum now on the right continue onto Mill Street , passing the church and the Bushel and Strike public house, to cross a small bridge over the stream by converted mill buildings. Keep with the road to the left at the next junction, heading away from the

Steeple Morden church

village, to a T-junction where **turn L** then keep right, heading for Steeple Morden and over the boundary into Cambridgeshire.

At the next junction on a left bend **turn R with care**, again signed for Steeple Morden. Continue with a windmill in view to the left and on into Steeple Morden and a T-junction with Station Road where **turn L**. Pass the church, parish well, and the Waggon and Horses to return to the parking on the left.

• •

PARISH WELL, STEEPLE MORDEN
Just by the Waggon and Horses and now rather overgrown, this well was in use until 1936 when piped water came. Legend has it that when the church steeple fell around 1620, the spire penetrated the earth at this point and formed the well.

GUILDEN MORDEN
This was once known as Golden Morden. In the 1800s it enjoyed a population boom and relative prosperity when it became a centre for the extraction of coprolite, an early fertiliser. The population then fell as the industry was superseded by Chilean imports.

ASHWELL QUARRY NATURE RESERVE
Here, flower-rich grassland in an old chalk pit is maintained by the Hertfordshire and Middlesex Wildlife Trust. Access to the quarry is via permit only, which can be gained by calling the warden on 01462 742684 after 6 pm.

ASHWELL
The village owes both its name and its existence to the springs found at the eastern end of Main Street. These give birth to the River Rhee, which later becomes the Cam. The village was initially inhabited in the Iron Age. There is evidence of hut circles, visible from air, which were built within the hill fort that commanded the Icknield Way.

ASHWELL VILLAGE MUSEUM
This museum is maintained by local people and is in the Town House. The building is now an ancient monument and contains artefacts that portray the history of the village from prehistoric days to the present, with many examples of tools used by farmers, shepherds, blacksmiths and other tradesmen.

9

Fen Drayton Nature Reserve and the Great Ouse

Off-road circuit: 2½ miles
Road circuit: 15 miles

Two routes for the price of one starting out from the Fen Drayton Nature Reserve by the River Great Ouse. First, or second as you please, a short off-road ride around the nature reserve and along the riverbank, followed by a quiet circuit on minor roads close to the busy A14, including a visit to Hilton and its 17th-century turf maze.

Maps: OS Landranger 153 and 154 Bedford and Huntingdon, and Cambridge and Newmarket (GR 339690).

Starting point: Fen Drayton Nature Reserve, to the north of the A14 and east of Fenstanton. Parking is available.

By train: There is no suitable rail station for this route.

Refreshments: Elsworth has the Poacher, a freehouse with an attractive beer garden, and the George and Dragon, also a freehouse with an outdoor seating area. In Boxworth the Golden Ball Inn serves food all day Sunday and has an outdoor area.

The route: The nature reserve circuit is an ideal introduction to off-road riding for children, but do take care along the riverbank. The surface is good, and should be pleasant all year round though there will be some mud to contend with after wet weather in winter. The accompanying road route is mostly on quiet lanes, but there are a couple of crossings of the busy A14 and a stretch of the B1040 that requires care.

For the off-road circuit: From the parking area follow the grassy track into the nature reserve and at a junction go straight ahead and to the left on the bridleway. This follows the water's edge, keeping between the water and the concrete road just to the left. The concrete road could be followed as an alternative though the waterside track is much more pleasant.

After crossing a couple of bridges the end of the lake is reached and a bridleway junction, where **turn R.** The bridleway narrows and becomes a little more overgrown, but still with no difficulties, before

45

Fen Drayton Nature Reserve

climbing slightly to the riverbank where **turn R**. Continue along the beautiful riverbank with views to the left of the church and meadows of Holywell. At the point where the Ferry Boat Inn can be tantalisingly viewed across the river, **turn R** on Ferry Boat Lane. Unless a passing boat can be flagged down, or the ferry comes back into service, that drink will have to wait until later!

The rough track turns to better road conditions, passing a lake on the left and, just after a tarmac road goes to the right, **turn R** onto the bridleway going back into Fen Drayton Nature Reserve. This leads along the water's edge to a bridge and the junction visited earlier in the day, where **turn L** to return to the car park.

For the main route: Follow the potholed track from the car parking back towards Fen Drayton. At the edge of the village ignore the right turn on Daintrees Road and continue on to High Street. **Turn R** at the next junction for Fenstanton and St Ives, then keep with the road at a sharp left bend onto Mill Road and out of the village.

Just before reaching the 'give way' at the busy A14, **turn R**, signed 'Cycle path to Fenstanton'. Continue with the cycle path but

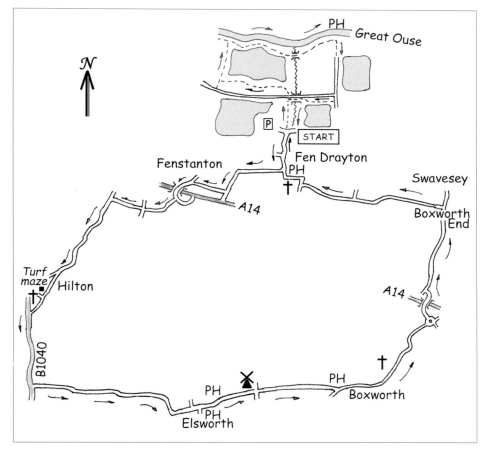

rejoin the road before the next junction where **turn L**, signed for Connington and Hilton. After crossing over the A14 **turn R**, again signed for Connington and Hilton.

Go straight on at a minor crossroads and at a 'give way' **turn L**, signed for Hilton, onto a winding road that leads between tall trees and hedgerows into the village. Pass by pretty cottages and the cricket pavilion followed by the turf maze and information board

just before the green on the right. The road then leads through a ford, which can be avoided by a footbridge to the right if necessary, by the church to a 'give way' with the busier B1040 where **turn L**.

Follow the B road for just over 1 mile, where **turn L** for Elsworth and Boxworth. If you meet the A1198 you've gone too far! The road climbs with opening views to the left before descending into the village of Elsworth through a series

The turf maze at Hilton

of bends. Keep straight ahead through the village, passing the Poacher, then over the bridge in the valley bottom to climb out of the village, passing the George and Dragon, with the old windmill in view ahead.

Continue straight on at the junction, heading for Boxworth. In Boxworth continue into the village, passing the Golden Ball Inn freehouse and restaurant on the left.

Keep with the road then leaving the village with the church on the left away hidden in the trees. A windy road leads to a roundabout where **turn L**, heading for Swavesey, to cross back over the A14. At the 'give way' **turn R**, signed for Swavesey and Over. **Take great care** at busy times on these junctions near the A14.

The road leads into Swavesey, with Boxworth End Farm on the left. At the next junction **turn L**, signed for Fen Drayton, just before the telephone box on the right on Rose and Crown Road. There are views to the old windmill and to Swavesey away to the right. Carry on to Fen Drayton where **turn R** at the 'give way' on Honey Hill and into the village. Pass the war memorial on the left and bear right

There are good tracks through the nature reserve at Fen Drayton

by the Three Tuns onto High Street where continue straight ahead to return to the parking at the nature reserve.

• •

FEN DRAYTON NATURE RESERVE

Sited on old gravel workings, this has become one of the most important areas for bird watching in Cambridgeshire. Some 213 different species have been recorded in the area since 1953, with 65 of these found to be breeding on site. There are a number of information boards around the reserve giving access details.

THE OLDE FERRRY BOAT INN

Although out of reach whilst cycling the route, this ancient hostelry is worth a visit. Not only does it have an excellent reputation for food but it is also steeped in history. As the oldest inn in England, as documented in the *Guinness Book of Records*, the first alcohol was sold on site around AD 560. For hundreds of years a ferry was operational, carrying its passengers from the inn across the River Ouse to Over. Legend has it that Hereward the Wake used its services when escaping the Normans at Madingley.

THE TURF MAZE, HILTON

This was created in 1660 by William Sparrow as evidenced by the monument at the centre of the maze. It is one of only eight turf mazes remaining in England and was recently restored by English Heritage.

10

Shepreth, Fowlmere and Duxford

20 miles

A very full day out is offered by this ride around the rolling countryside just to the south of Cambridge. Starting out from Shepreth, with its wildlife park, there is an opportunity to visit the wonderful Fowlmere Nature Reserve – and then there is the Imperial War Museum at Duxford, still only halfway around the route! The latter part of the ride is no less interesting, passing through some of the most picturesque, and wealthy, of Cambridgeshire villages. Barrington, near the end of the ride, is particularly attractive with its broad green and thatched cottages.

Map: OS Landranger 154 Cambridge and Newmarket (GR 392482).

Starting point: Shepreth railway station, where there is a small amount of parking available. Alternatively, you could park at Fowlmere Nature Reserve or by the riverside just to the north-west of Shepreth. Both Fowlmere and Shepreth are reached from the A10 between Royston and junction 11 of the M11.

By train: Shepreth or Whittlesford.

Refreshments: As you are never far from a settlement there are plenty of pubs and shops on or just off this route. Being at about the halfway point, Duxford and Whittlesford are both good choices. Just on the route in Duxford, the Plough serves food from Tuesday to Saturday and at Sunday lunchtime. There are further pubs and shops just off the route in the village. In Whittlesford you come to the Tickell Arms, a place to go if you feel like splashing out, followed by the Bees in the Wall.

The route: A full day out, especially if time is taken to visit Fowlmere Nature Reserve and the Imperial War Museum at Duxford. This ride also involves several busy road crossings, so is more suited to the experienced cyclist.

From the station **turn L** and continue through the village on Fowlmere Road to a junction with the busy A10. Go straight ahead here, **with great care**, heading for Fowlmere. In approximately 1 mile, by a small church and cemetery, turn R, signed for Melbourn and Royston and the RSPB Visitor Centre, and a little way along the single-track road **turn L**, again signed for the RSPB. This leads to the Fowlmere Nature Reserve and parking.

Fowlmere Nature Reserve

After visiting the nature reserve, go back to the T-junction and **turn R** to return to the small church where, again, **turn R**, heading for Fowlmere. In the village at the 'give way' by the Queen's Head, **turn R** onto the B1368 and where the road then bends to the right, and just before a caravan park, **turn L** onto Pipers Close, signed for the village hall. Pass a pumping station on the right and arrive at a junction with the A505 where **turn R** and **immediately L with great care**, signed for Chrishall Grange and Crishall. The minor road then leads between open fields to a junction at Chrishall Grange. **Turn L** here and at the next junction **turn R**, signed for Duxford.

The road leads very pleasantly, passing Duxford Grange on the left and open fields to the right, in more or less a straight line with several dips and climbs. Then, with Duxford airfield and the Imperial War Museum in view to the left, cross over the M11 by a bridge to a crossroads on the edge of Duxford. Straight ahead here leads to the Plough and on into Duxford, with shops and further refreshment opportunities.

Turn L at the crossroads and follow the traffic-calmed road towards a roundabout, joining the cyclepath

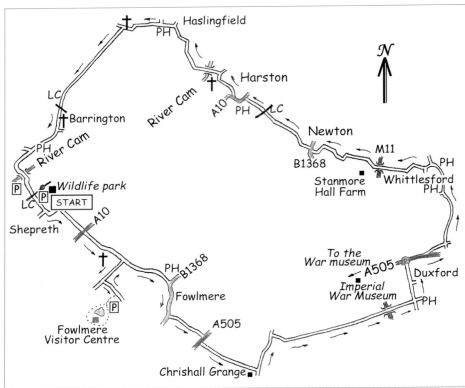

to the left. At the roundabout dismount and cross to the cyclepath on the other side, which runs by the side of the busy A505. Left here leads via a combination of cycle and footpath over a busy junction with the M11 to the Imperial War Museum. **Turn R** to continue the route, heading for Whittlesford.

The cycle route shortly branches away from the A505 to follow the old road and at a junction where the station is straight ahead, **turn L** into Whittlesford. Continue, passing the playground and green,

and ride on through the village by an impressive timber-framed building on the right and the Tickell Arms on the left. On leaving the village pass a further pub, the Bees in the Wall, and **turn L** at the next junction, signed for Newton and Harston. Keep right at the next junction on Newton Road to re-cross the motorway, noting the information board to the left just over the bridge.

Continue then through a series of bends into Newton and up to a 'give way' where **take care** and **turn R**, then **immediately L**,

The Tickell Arms, Whittlesford

signed for Harston. Pass a shop on the left and continue out of Newton up Harston Hill to then descend to a level crossing and on to a junction with the busy A10 in Harston just past the Pemberton Arms. **Turn L** and then shortly **turn R with great care**, signed for Haslingfield. Note that there is a shared-use cyclepath on the right if required.

Pass the church on the left and keep with the main road leaving the village to cross over the River Cam. Keep right with the road by Charity Farm and climb to Haslingfield. Follow the main road through the village, passing the Little Rose public house on the left, the village shop on the right and, at the church, **turn L** onto Chapel Hill.

Climb now more steeply before the road levels out and descends with impressive views ahead and a cement works on the right. Cross the unguarded level crossing by the cement works, keeping an eye out for trains, and continue into Barrington. Note that there is a 'cycle gate' to the left of the speed restrictions on entering the village to ease the passage of cyclists.

After passing the church on the left, keep with the road to the right by the green, passing pretty thatched cottages, a converted chapel and other attractive buildings in the village. There is a shop on the left and towards the end of the green the thatched Royal Oak. Continue straight on at the end of the green, signed for Shepreth, and follow the road as it bends sharp left and over the Cam. To the right a car park gives access to a riverside meadowland walk and the road shortly leads back to Shepreth.

SHEPRETH WILDLIFE PARK
Starting life in 1979 as a refuge for injured and orphaned British birds and mammals, this is now home to a wide variety of wildlife such as monkeys and tigers. There is also a reptile house, a pets' corner, a café, a shop and play areas. It is open 10 am to 6 pm every day, or till dusk in the winter.

FOWLMERE NATURE RESERVE
Allow an hour for a reasonable look around this wonderful wildlife haven, which has a visitor centre, public conveniences, a very pleasant picnic area and also a bike rack. Bikes are not allowed in the reserve but it is well worth parking up and walking to some of the bird hides, where you may be lucky enough to spot a kingfisher or an otter! A nature trail wanders around the reed beds and mere where a great deal of animal and plant life can be seen, in addition to the numerous species of birds.

IMPERIAL WAR MUSEUM
The museum stands on a historic airfield and is home to a collection of over 200 aircraft ranging from First World War bi-planes to current combat aircraft. In addition, it has one of the finest collections of tanks, military vehicles and artillery in Britain. It is open from 10 am to 6 pm in the summer and 10 am to 4 pm in the winter, with a variety of special exhibitions throughout the year.

STANMORE HALL FARM
Part of Cambridgeshire County Council's county farms estate, this is included in the Department of the Environment's countryside stewardship scheme which encourages traditional farming methods and landscapes.

BARRINGTON VILLAGE
Surely one of the prettiest villages in Cambridgeshire with its thatched cottages and large green, where local schoolchildren used to dance around the maypole on May Day. Villagers could graze their cows and horses for ten shillings a year; goats and geese were free!

Willingham, Histon and the Fen Edge

19 miles

Restored village pumps and a thatched church are among the highlights of this round of popular villages just beyond the outskirts of Cambridge. There is also the chance to visit the Red Lion at Histon, a must for fans of real ale and the traditional public house.

Map: OS Landranger 154 Cambridge and Newmarket (GR 408705).

Starting point: In the centre of Willingham by the village sign and restored pump on the green, where there is a parking area. The village is on the B1050, which runs between the A1123 at Earith and the A14 north-west of Cambridge.

By train: Waterbeach, on the Cambridge to Ely line, from where the route can easily be joined at Landbeach in just over 1 mile.

Refreshments: There are pubs, shops and cafés in many of the villages on the route, along with numerous village greens and open public areas for picnicking. If a pub stop is to be made, the Red Lion freehouse at Histon is highly recommended, and is about halfway round.

The route: A generally flat route with some undulations, on mainly quiet roads with just a couple of busier sections in the larger villages where there are generally cycleway facilities. One off-road section is used, and the initial part of this can be quite muddy and rutted but it soon improves. The route between Longstanton and Oakington, which is shown on the OS map as track, is, in fact, good tarmac road with a traffic restriction.

From the parking in Willingham **turn L** to skirt round the green and then follow Church Street, passing the Duke of Wellington pub followed by the Three Tuns, shops and church. At a junction by the Co-op **turn L**, pass more shops and the post office then, at the traffic lights, **turn R**, signed for Over.

Just after leaving the village, pass Highgate Country Store and Craft Centre on the right and then climb slightly with a water tower, windmill and communication mast in view to the left. On entering Over, take the **first L** on Mill Road and wind amongst houses to a junction by the Exhibition pub and restaurant. **Turn L**, taking care around the parked cars, and at the next T-junction **turn L** again, on

Cycling through Longstanton

Longstanton Road. This leads by the village pond and shortly the windmill in the shadow of the communications mast.

Cross the disused railway and then descend slightly through bends. Ignore a right turn for Swavesey and Fen Drayton, to arrive at a T-junction in Longstanton. **Turn R with care** onto the B1050. Pass the Black Bull Chinese restaurant and where the B road turns to the right, continue straight ahead, noting the shared-use cycle path on the left if required. At a junction by the church **turn L** and **immediately R** on Woodside, signed for Caravans and Camping and as a 'no through road'. Shortly pass the thatched church, St Michael's, on the left and on leaving the village keep with the minor road as it becomes restricted for motor vehicles. This shortly leads to Oakington. Pass the White Horse pub on the left and shops on the right to arrive at traffic lights, where make use of the cycle advance start lane and go straight ahead.

The road now is relatively quiet, but there is a shared-use cycle path on the left if required, which leads in a little under 1 mile to a minor junction where **turn L**, signed for Impington and Histon. After a level crossing over a disused railway, a sharp right bend leads into Histon. Keep right at a minor junction, and then **turn R** onto a more major road, which then passes the Red Lion.

Continue passing further shops and pubs, and on the left the village green, pond and pump (restored in 1984) to the traffic lights where **turn R** and **immediately L**, signed for Impington and Milton.

The road leads to Impington, with no break in the built-up area, passing St Andrew's church on the left and then continuing through a sharp right bend. On leaving the village after a further sharp right, pass the entrance track to Bedlam Farm and, shortly, by Mere Way Farm **turn L** on a byway, which crosses the road. The initially muddy track proceeds through the fruit farm, following the line of the Roman Ackerman Street.

Beyond the fruit farm the track

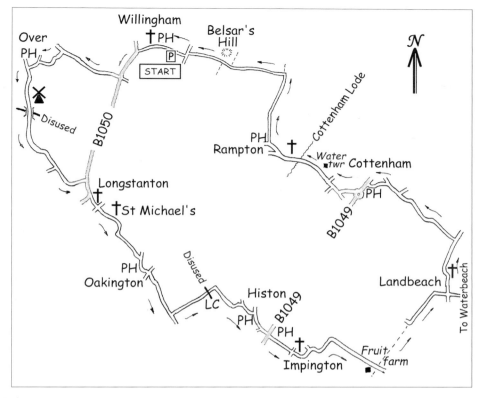

improves and becomes grassy, before turning a little muddy once more on arriving at the minor road by Punch Farm. Continue straight ahead on the road, and then through a sharp right bend to arrive in Landbeach by the car park, village hall and playing field. At the crossroads **turn L**, signed for Ely, Stretham and Cottenham, pass pretty thatched cottages and the church on the right, then shortly after leaving the village **turn L**, signed for Cottenham.

The road leads between open fields and then a series of bends into Cottenham. Keep with the road to the left, signed for Histon, to arrive at a 'give way' by the war memorial and Chequers pub. **Turn L** and shortly at a mini-roundabout **turn R**, signed for Rampton, Oakington and Willingham. Then, at the other side of the green, **turn R again** on Rampton Road.

At the next junction go straight on where the Oakington road goes to the left and pass an old water tower to the right; note the shared-use cycleway if required. Leave Cottenham, descending slightly, and cross over the Cottenham Lode

St Michael's church, Longstanton

to arrive in Rampton. Where the road bends to the left keep right, heading for Willingham, and then **turn R** just before the pub and by the chapel onto Cow Lane.

The road leads by a caravan site on the right and occasional farm buildings, the surface becoming broken after a right bend. Keep left at a 90° bend by a small orchard where the farm track to Iram Farm continues straight ahead. After passing a few houses, a muddy byway, often used by travellers, crosses the road via a staggered junction, and where the byway goes to the left, through a gate on the right the earthworks of an ancient hill fort, Belsar's Hill, are clearly visible in the field. The road then leads into Willingham and a 'give way' where **turn L** and **immediately R** by the village green and parking.

● ●

ST MICHAEL'S CHURCH, LONGSTANTON

This is maintained by the Redundant Churches Fund. There is an information board inside giving details of the re-thatching, which took place in 1955 and in 2000. In the grounds of the church is St Michael's well, which dates from medieval times and was formerly used for baptisms.

St Michael's well, Longstanton

THE RED LION, HISTON

Set up as a shrine to real ale and the traditional pub, an excellent selection of ales is always available here. The interior walls are covered in drinking memorabilia and one half of the bar ceiling features an unusual collection of water jugs, while the other half has a selection of font heads. There are also pub mirrors advertising various ales past and present, along with a collection of photographs and sketches connected with the pub and its history.

COTTENHAM WATER TOWER

The reason that this looks more like a windmill is that it began life as Tower Mill, being used from 1843–98 for processing cereals. In 1904 its cap was removed and this listed building took on its new role of water tower.

VILLAGE PUMPS, WILLINGHAM AND HISTON

In both villages the pumps are easily spotted as they are placed at the top of a small flight of steps on their relative greens, presumably to enable large receptacles to be placed under the pump and filled with water.

From Peat Fen to Salt Marsh and The Wash

27 miles

Leaving the small village of Tydd St Giles, the surroundings soon take on a remote and rural feel as this route leads us away from the relatively recently drained peat fen to a more ancient landscape of silt fen and salt marsh around the edges of The Wash, a national nature reserve. The Fens are often thought of as flat and uninteresting, with little to offer but solitude and big sky. This they certainly have, but as this ride will show there is much more: ancient settlements, traces of medieval salt workings, and magnificent medieval churches reflecting a more prosperous past at the centre of foreign trade.

Map: OS Landranger 131 Boston and Spalding (GR 427167).

Starting point: The route is described from the centre of Tydd St Giles by the church, post office and village shop. There is plenty of roadside parking. The village lies on the B1165 to the west of the A1101 north of Wisbech.

By train: There is no suitable train station for this route.

Refreshments: In Long Sutton, the Butterfly Park has an excellent café catering for visitors to the park, and there are also several shops and pubs. The Ship, which is the closest to the route, is very welcoming, serves food and has a pleasant outdoor seating area. There are also pubs in Lutton (the Jolly Crispin), which is probably best placed for 'halfway' refreshment – though food is only available at weekends – and Gedney Dyke (the Chequers), a place to go for a special treat. In Fleet Hargate the Willow Tea Rooms and Chestnut Farm both serve good food.

The route: Although this is a relatively long route, it covers more or less flat terrain, making the going fairly easy – dependent on wind direction! There are a couple of very easy and pleasant off-road sections, which should be passable even in very wet weather. Although primarily on minor roads, a couple of busy road crossings are made over the A17, so take care with children.

Set off in a northerly direction, with the church on your right, **keep L** with the road and then **turn R** leaving the village, signed for Sutton St James, on the B1165, Cat's Lane and National Cycle Network Route 1. Ignore a left turn on the B1165, continuing on Low

Guy's Head by the River Nene

Gate, which is followed into Tydd St Mary, ignoring minor junctions and the right-hand turn for National Cycle Network Route 1. At a T-junction with a busier road **turn L** and almost immediately **R with care** onto Cross Gate, heading for Sutton Crosses.

Continue, crossing the South Holland Main Drain, to a left-hand bend where **turn R** onto the more minor road with Long Sutton church spire visible ahead. Ignore the first left turn and where the road then bends right, just past the telephone box, **turn L** (easy to miss). At the A17 **turn L** and **immediately R with extreme care**
onto Seagate Road; dismount and cross on foot, if necessary.

Continue to a busier road in Long Sutton where a left turn leads to Long Sutton church and shops, but **turn R** and then shortly before the Ship Inn and duck pond **turn L**, signed for the Butterfly Park. Pass a derelict windmill on the right and take the **first R** onto Woad Lane, or continue straight on for a visit to the Butterfly Park.

A long straight section, with striking views of the gas-turbine power station and Sutton Bridge Docks, leads to a couple of bends and then a junction by King John

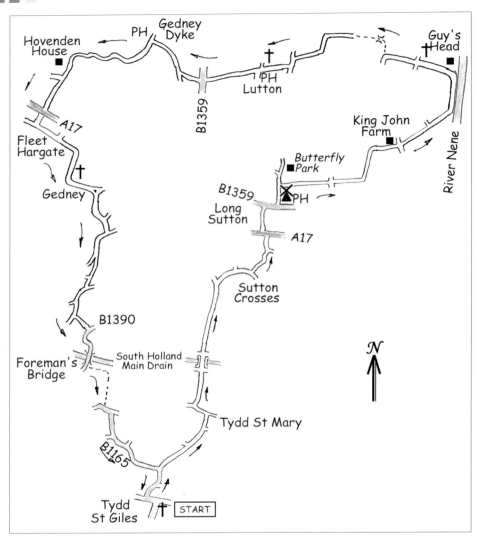

Farm where go straight across, signed for Gedney Drove End. Continue as the road climbs to join the west bank of the River Nene to arrive at Guy's Head.

Continue on the road following the old sea bank, with the new sea bank visible to the right and at the junction by a Methodist chapel, go straight on, following South Drove. At a 90° left bend **turn R** onto the rough bridleway, which shortly turns left, crosses a bridge and then follows a track to emerge on a minor road. This leads via a couple of bends to a junction where **turn L** and then **almost immediately R** by St Martin's Vestment into Lutton. Pass the church and the Jolly Crispin pub and continue out of the village, ignoring minor turns, to a junction with the B1359 where go straight ahead on Kings Gate. At the junction with Low Gate **turn R** and into Gedney Dyke, where **turn L** in front of the Chequers.

Leave Gedney Dyke and pass Hovenden House on the right, **take care** here as there is an HGV access road to a packing plant. At the junction with the busy A17, dismount and join the pavement on the right to cross the A17 and join the minor road behind the safety barrier opposite.

Follow the minor road and at the junction **turn L**, now following National Cycle Network Route 1. Pass the Willow Stores and Tea Rooms on the left, and shortly after a right-hand bend the teashop at the Chestnut Farm.

Follow the National Cycle Network Route 1 signs through Gedney and shortly after passing the impressive church, take a right-hand fork and then **turn R** again onto Stone Gate. Keep with the road at a right-hand bend and at a T-junction **turn R**, still following National Cycle Network Route 1. At the next junction **bear L**, again following National Cycle Network Route 1, onto Hunts Gate, heading for

Gedney church – the Cathedral of the Fens

Sutton St James. Ignore the minor road to the right, and shortly, at the next junction, **turn R**, now leaving National Cycle Network Route 1, but still heading for Sutton St James.

Pass a right turn and at the next junction **turn L** onto the more minor road, which leads to the busier B1390 where **turn R with care**. Continue through the S bends, cross Foreman's Bridge and immediately **turn L** onto the bridleway by the side of Foreman`s Bridge Caravan Park, which has a small shop and tourist information point. Follow the bridleway alongside the South Holland Main Drain and, where the drain turns to the left, continue more or less straight ahead to leave the bank side and follow a rough trail.

At the end of the track **turn L** on the B road and almost immediately at a junction **turn R with care**, signed for Tydd St Giles. Keep with the road, passing a couple of minor junctions, to a 'give way' where **turn R with care**, as the bend to the right is partly obscured. Continue, passing a golf course on the left, and so back into Cambridgeshire to return to Tydd St Giles once more on National Cycle Network Route 1.

• •

SOUTH HOLLAND MAIN DRAIN
Built in 1763, this is the largest watercourse in the area. It was improved in 1942 during the Second World War as large areas of pasture were ploughed to grow corn and so additional drainage was needed. Following a serious flood in 1968 further improvements were made in the form of five new pumping stations.

BUTTERFLY PARK, LONG SUTTON
Open late March to late October. The tropical house is home to butterflies, birds and various reptiles, and there is also a fascinating ant room. At around 12 noon and 3 pm most days an extremely entertaining falconry display takes place featuring a variety of birds, from the comical turkey vulture to the graceful peregrine falcon. An animal centre, an adventure playground, a wildlife walk, a gift shop and an especially good licensed tea room make this a great place to visit.

KING JOHN FARM
This is the alleged spot where King John, in 1216, famously lost his baggage in The Wash. His baggage train, risking life, limb and cargo, attempted a crossing of the treacherous Cross Keys Wash. Struggling through mud and poorly defined tracks

they did, in fact, lose most of their precious load, which is still thought to be hidden deep in the mud. This remained a dangerous crossing until 1831 when the newly-constructed five-span oak bridge with its core of iron allowed the first vehicle to cross safely into Sutton Bridge. A further bridge, built in 1862, was finally replaced by the present day version, built between 1894 and 1897, which uses the same powering mechanism as the Tower Bridge in London.

GUY'S HEAD
The twin lighthouses that make Guy's Head easily recognisable have been converted to domestic dwellings, but once marked the entrance of the Nene from The Wash. The footpath from the parking area leads out along the Nene to The Wash and the salt marshes, with views over to the right of the North Norfolk coast. This is an area where seals can often be seen after a high tide.

SALTERNS
Keep an eye out around Gedney Dyke and Hovenden House for long, low mounds in the fields – the remains of medieval salt mining. The salt marshes and tidal estuaries of this area provided ideal conditions for the extensive salt production that took place around this time.

ST MARY MAGDALENE, GEDNEY
Known locally as the Cathedral of the Fens, this church, with its rare medieval entrance door, is indeed an impressive sight. Its two great tiers of windows, the lower being 14th century, the upper early Tudor, are so large and clear that they give the building an almost transparent appearance.

13

The Outskirts of Wisbech: Cambridgeshire's Cider Country

14 or 23 miles

Starting out from Friday Bridge, this ride on quiet fenland lanes passes among apple orchards and agricultural fields, visiting on the way Marmont Priory Lock on the Nene-Ouse Navigation Link, one of the few locks required in the flat lands of the Fens. There is also the opportunity to extend the route with a visit to the old Green Bank Pumping Station, now a Drainage Museum – though not often open to the public this makes a worthwhile diversion just for the pleasant cycling.

Map: OS Landranger 143 Ely and Wisbech (GR 465046).

Starting point: Friday Bridge, on the B1101 south of Wisbech. There is a small amount of parking near the Clock Tower and by the Chequers Inn.

By train: There is no suitable train station for this route.

Refreshments: The Chequers and the Bridge in Friday Bridge serve bar snacks. There are also pubs and shops just off the route in Upwell and Outwell and towards the end of the route in Emneth, including the intriguingly-named Gaultree Inn.

The route: A typically flat fenland ride on quiet lanes, but with a couple of busy road crossings. The shorter route would make an ideal introductory or family ride on a day with good weather, but particular care is needed on the two crossings of the A1101.

From the parking area cross the road **with care** and take Well End towards the post office, signed for Upwell. Pass the Bridge public house and at a minor junction **turn R** onto Laddus Drove. A long straight road then leads in approximately 2 miles to a sharp left bend where the road meets the river.

Continue along the riverbank, passing a small apple orchard on the left, then Marmont Priory Lock on the right. Continue into the outskirts of Upwell, where **turn L** on Thurlands Drove, heading away from the river and the village. Note: Straight on here would lead into Upwell with its pubs and shops, but if you do this detour

The Ouse-Nene link on the outskirts of Upwell

take care once you reach the busier road.

The rough single-track road of Thurlands Drove passes several orchards both small and large and a mixture of residential and agricultural properties leading after 1½ miles to a T-junction by another orchard where **turn L**. Pass the phone box and **turn R**, signed for Outwell, passing a post box on the left.

On approaching the busy A1101 keep with the minor road to the right to arrive at a junction where **turn L**, and then go straight across **with care** at the junction with the A road, signed for Marshland St James. There is a small shop at the filling station just to the left at this junction.

Continue to a 'give way' where **turn L**, and at the next junction keep right with the road. After a series of Z-bends **turn L** in Emneth Hungate, heading towards Emneth on Hungate Road to return directly to Friday Bridge (see below).

Alternatively, for the circular route to Green Bank Pumping Station: Shortly afterwards **turn R** onto Moyses Bank. Continue straight on at a minor crossroad to a 'give way' where **turn L**, then at the next junction, by another small orchard, **turn R**, signed for Middle Drove and Stow Bridge. Keep left with the road at a bend over Forty Foot Bridge and just past a right turn for Outwell, **turn L**, signed for Tilney St Lawrence, on Middle Drove.

After a Z-bend, the road bends left over the river and leads to a junction where **turn R** to see the Green Bank Pumping Station and Drainage Museum. Then retrace your steps but now follow National Cycle Network Route 1, **turning L** into Tilney Fen End on Chapel Road, passing the converted chapel on the right. Keep with the road as it zig zags over the river to a junction where **turn L**, still on National Cycle Network Route 1, signed for Marshland St James and Emneth, along The Smeeth.

Continue straight on where National Cycle Network Route 1 turns to the right for Walpole Highway and straight on again at the next crossroads. The route then

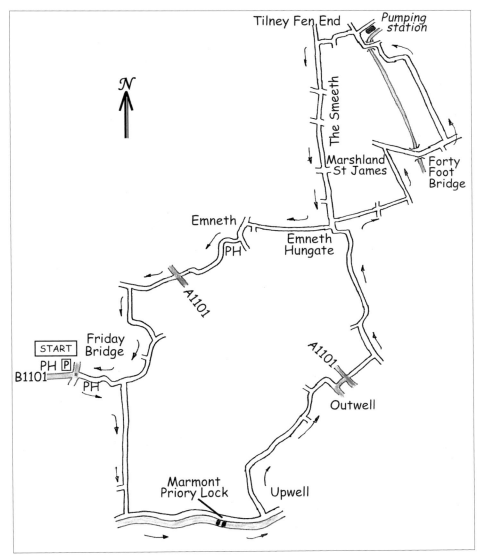

leads via several more orchards back to Emneth Hungate, ignoring another minor crossroads. In Emneth Hungate **turn R**, signed for Emneth, on Hungate Road, now back on the original route.

To complete both routes: In Emneth continue to the 'give way', where **turn L**, passing the post office and general store. Shortly **turn R with care** by the Gaultree Inn onto The Wroe. Ignore minor junctions and eventually arrive at a junction with the busy A road, where go straight across **with care** onto Colletts Bridge. Continue onto Gosmore Lane and shortly after passing Fenmarc **turn L** at a minor junction by a bridge over the dyke. After a sharp left bend this leads to a junction where **turn R**, which leads back onto Well End and into Friday Bridge, the water tower being clearly visible all the way.

One of the two towers in Friday Bridge

FRIDAY BRIDGE INTERNATIONAL FARM CAMP

This was built on the March road towards the end of the Second World War to accommodate prisoners of war, who were set to work on the land. It is presently used to house agricultural workers. The information board by the parking area gives details.

THE TWIN TOWER CYCLE ROUTE

The Friday Bridge information board also describes this route, which, although it includes a good traffic-free stretch, is rather spoilt by a long, often busy, section on the B1101.

WATER TOWER, FRIDAY BRIDGE

Built in 1894, the first in the Fens area, this holds 100,000 gallons of water.

MARMONT PRIORY LOCK

Part of the Nene-Ouse Navigation Link, which is the recommended route between the rivers Nene and Ouse. It follows a 28½ mile course from the Nene near Peterborough to the Ouse at Denver Sluice via Whittlesey and March.

GREEN BANK PUMPING STATION

Like many similar installations throughout the Fens, this was used to lift water into the river course above to maintain drainage. Now no longer in use it is a Drainage Museum, but currently open to the public on just a few days a year.

EMNETH VICARAGE

Revd W. Audry, the author of the *Thomas the Tank Engine* books, was vicar at St Edmunds in Emneth from 1953 to 1965 and wrote his last few books at the vicarage. 'Thomas' was recently commemorated in a stained-glass window in the church.

Welches Dam and the Hundred Foot Washes

16 miles

A delight for birdwatchers and lovers of wild places alike, the Welches Dam Visitor Centre by the Ouse Washes Nature Reserve serves as our starting point for this circuit around open fens with a visit to Britain's lowest hill fort. The nature reserve has several bird hides and pleasant waterside walks – a must to explore before or after your ride. In winter when the washes are flooded the views are often very dramatic.

Map: OS Landranger 143 Ely and Wisbech (GR 470861).

Starting point: The visitor centre at Welches Dam, where there is ample parking. This is reached from the B1093 south of Manea.

By train: The route passes through Manea, which is served by trains from Peterborough, Ely, Thetford and Norwich.

Refreshments: The Ship Inn at Purl's Bridge near the start and end of the route is recommended, and is open at lunchtime through to the evening on Sunday, with food available. During the week it is open evenings only, from 5.30 pm. Manea has several shops and food outlets.

The route: This follows minor roads and there is also a long bridleway section, which may be muddy in parts during winter but is mostly on a good surface. If necessary the bridleway can be avoided by continuing on the road into Manea and returning via the outward route. Two B roads are used and the B1098 in particular, while not busy, is prone to speeding traffic. Good visibility means this should not cause any great problem, but as ever do take care.

From the visitor centre car park follow the road towards Manea, passing wetlands on the right in front of the Ouse river bank, then the Ship Inn on the left. After approximately 2 miles, at a junction **turn R** onto Straight Road, signed for Manea. Ignore a right turn at a sharp left bend, pass the playing field on the right and at a T-junction with the main road **turn R** opposite the Rose and Crown.

Follow the B1093 through Manea, heading towards the station. At a

Looking along the Sixteen Foot Drain at Boot's Bridge

junction, with the station and level crossing just ahead, **turn L**, signed for Wimblington Marsh and Chatteris, still on the B1093. Bends by a group of farms lead to a long straight section of road across open fenland below, with views ahead and to the right of Wimblington grain store on the very slightly higher ground that includes Stonea Camp. This is the hill fort that we will visit shortly.

At a crossroads by Boot's Bridge Farm continue straight ahead and over Boot's Bridge. Shortly **turn R**, signed for Stonea Camp Iron Age Fort, on a rough tarmac road that leads via Stitches Farm to the hill

fort. A gate by a small, corrugated iron-roofed building gives access, and information boards around the site tell the story and include plans of the area in Iron Age times.

After visiting the hill fort return by Stitches Farm to the road and **turn L** back to Boots Bridge, where **turn R** on the B1098, heading for Chatteris. Continue alongside the Sixteen Foot Drain, passing sluices old and new and several bridges. Follow the road as it bends left where two watercourses meet and just before a right-hand bend **turn L** on Byall Fen Drive, heading for Manea.

After a couple of bends and after

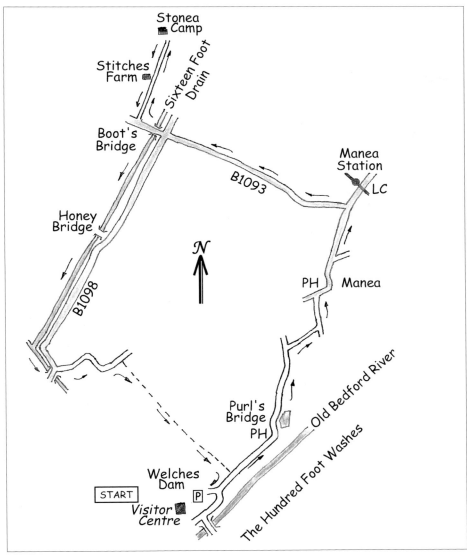

passing the entrance to Honey Hill Farm on the left, **turn R with care** onto a public bridleway by a gravel layby and a clump of trees. After a short distance the grassy bridleway turns to a gravel track for a while before becoming once more grassy and a little more rutted by old farm buildings. The bridleway continues on more or less the same straight line throughout to reach the minor road used earlier where **turn R** to return to Welches Dam and the car parking, or left to visit the Ship Inn.

The Washes in winter, with the bridge under water

OUSE WASHES NATURE RESERVE

This is now the largest area of regularly flooded washland in Britain and as such is a haven for wildlife. In winter it attracts many species of ducks and swans, with redshanks, snipe and lapwings breeding in spring. Dragonflies, damselflies and over 300 kinds of plants thrive in this Site of Special Scientific Interest. The car park, toilets and hides are always open and the visitor centre opens every day, 9 am to 5 pm, except Christmas Day and Boxing Day.

STONEA IRON AGE FORT

Protected from the north by many banks and ditches and from the south by fenland marshes and streams, this is the lowest hill fort in Britain. It was originally built in the Iron Age but was used in defence against the Romans. There are a number of information boards around the area detailing the history of the site. Modest though its elevation may be, when standing on the remaining defensive earthworks you can see it had quite a commanding view of the surrounding area.

STITCHES FARM

First recorded in 1251, the original farm appears to have been north of Stonea Camp as shown on the camp's information board maps. The name Stitches derives from 'stitch beche' meaning pieces of land and like Stonea refers specifically to gravelly marshland. The Domesday Book records that a grange for Doddington Manor, which was held by the Abbot of Ely, was situated on Stonea Island. This house, although an ancient building of great local interest, was demolished in 1873.

Hilly Byways to the West of the Isle of Ely

17½ miles

This ride follows a delightful mixture of off-road and quiet lanes in a rare hilly part of the Fens, visiting on the way villages that, like Ely, would once have sat on islands in the surrounding marshland. Views to the Isle of Ely itself, along with its magnificent cathedral, are never far away on this route, ranging from little more than a speck in the distance along the New Bedford River to an imposing backdrop on the approach to Little Downham.

Map: OS Landranger 143 Ely and Wisbech (GR 523838).

Starting point: Little Downham, where there is a public car park by the Plough on Tower Road leading to Park Lane. The village is on the B1411, which runs between the A10 north-west of Ely and the A1101.

By train: From Ely station, where the route can be joined on the outskirts of Ely as it climbs to Little Downham.

Refreshments: The Three Pickerels pub and restaurant in Mepal has a very pleasant riverside garden and is recommended. There are also pubs and shops in Little Downham.

The route: An ideal family summer outing. In winter some of the off-road sections used can be muddy, particularly the stretch from Witcham though this can be avoided by an on-road alternative which adds just a little over half a mile to the ride. Although this is a hilly area for the Fens, the land never rises much more than 60 ft above sea level, so any climbs are relatively short lived. However, the high percentage of off-road cycling will make this ride feel longer than the distance suggests.

At the junction by the Plough **turn R**, heading out of Little Downham on the B1411. Keep with the B road at the next junction where it bends right heading for Pymore and descends from the high ground. Pass Cophall Drove on the left, and at the next junction **turn L** on Adventurers' Drove, heading for Oxlode and marked as a 'no through road'. In Oxlode meet the riverbank and **turn L** on the private road, which is a public bridleway. The bank above

Cyclists on the Coveney Road

contains a footpath and the river with views over the Washes.

The bridleway now continues along the rough track at the base of the riverbank, with views to Ely Cathedral away in the distance to the left. After approximately 3 miles, by Byall Fen, the bridleway bends to the right and then shortly at Widdens Hill climbs slightly to run alongside the footpath and river. This leads to a road on the edge of Mepal by the now-redundant bridge over the New Bedford River; to the right is the Three Pickerels pub.

Unless visiting the pub **turn L** onto the road and keep with it as it winds through the village. On leaving Mepal, where the road bends right to join the A142, **turn L**, signed for Witcham and Coveney, on Witcham Road. Climb into Witcham, at the dizzy height of 62 ft above sea level, and keep right with the road by the cemetery. At the crossroads by the playing field **turn L** onto the High Street, passing the Old Manor House and church on the left.

At the T-junction with Headleys Lane **turn R**. The road then turns to byway and bears to the left. After an initial concrete stretch the surface becomes badly rutted; the

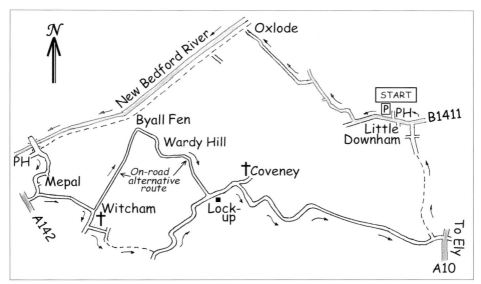

first section in particular would be very muddy in winter. The track improves in its latter part, becoming mainly grassy, and leads to a road where **turn L**. Follow the road to arrive in Coveney, passing the Old Town Lock-Up and an information board on the right.

To avoid this off-road section: On entering Witcham **turn L** by the cemetery and follow the road via Byall Fen and Wardy Hill to rejoin the main route on the edge of Coveney, where **turn L**.

Shortly after passing Manor Farm, **turn R** to descend on the road signed for Ely, heading directly for the cathedral, which dominates the view ahead. After a series of bends, and on approaching the outskirts of Ely and the busy A10, ignore the first byway on the left through a farmyard but just before the A road **turn L** onto Hurst Lane, marked as a 'no through road'. Initially on tarmac, the byway soon becomes rough and rutted, but never as bad as the byway from Witcham. Just after the worst section of track it reverts to tarmac. Ignore a byway to the left and stick with the tarmac to climb back to Little Downham.

Continue straight ahead on Chapel Lane on entering the village, and then at the junction with the B road **turn L**, passing the supermarket and post office to the pub and parking.

● ● ● ● ● ● ● ● ● ● ● ● ● ● ● ● ● ●

LITTLE DOWNHAM
The 'Downham' part of the name means 'home on the dunes' or 'settlement on the hills' – an apt description for this village, which was once a real island,

Ely Cathedral

surrounded by marshes. From 1286 until the development of housing in the 1960s there were many orchards and vineyards in the area.

THE THREE PICKERELS

Over a hundred years ago this unusually-named hotel and restaurant was just one of five public houses and a brewery in the village of Mepal. The name presumably related to the local pastime of fishing, as a pickerel is a young pike.

COVENEY OLD TOWN LOCK-UP

This was, in fact, used to house the village 'bier' which carried the coffins to church. Next to the lock-up is the village pound where cattle straying from common grazing areas were kept.

ELY

The name is derived from Elge – 'eel district' – and Elig – 'eel island' – referring to the large number of eels that used to be caught in the region. The city was built on an island above the Fens and the area is still known as the Isle of Ely.

ELY CATHEDRAL

The 'ship of the fens' is one of the largest cathedrals in England and provides a spectacular site for miles around. It is well worth a visit. Open all year round, there are free guided tours and evensong is sung daily (except Wednesday). The Refectory and Almonry restaurant provide home cooking using local produce. There is also an animal safari, maze, brass rubbing and souvenir shop.

Wicken Fen and the River Cam

17 miles

This ride combines a visit to the Wicken Fen Nature Reserve and Visitor Centre, which itself could easily take an hour or two to explore, with a circuit of the wider Adventurers' Fen. This whole area is steeped in drainage history with highlights including the water wind pump at Wicken Fen, sluices at Upware and the Burwell Lode through Burwell. Equally interesting, but making history more recently, is the Dyke's End pub in the historic village of Reach.

Map: OS Landranger 154 Cambridge and Newmarket (GR 564705).

Starting point: Wicken Fen Visitor Centre, where parking is available. This is just south of Wicken, which is on the A1123.

By train: No suitable rail starting point.

Refreshments: Early on the route, in Upware, the Five Miles pub has a very pretty setting on the River Cam with indoor and outdoor eating areas, then late on the route there is the Anchor in Burwell, which also serves food and has a riverside garden. However, at about the halfway point, and serving excellent food and drink, is the highly recommended Dykes End, in Reach. In Wicken at the end of the route the Maid's Head has an outdoor seating area on the Green. In addition, there are shops in Burwell and just off the route in Soham, plus the café at Wicken Fen Visitor Centre.

The route: Partly on quiet lanes, this route also includes sections of the B1102 and the A1123, and although not as busy as many major routes, it does make the ride unsuitable for inexperienced family groups or small children. Discussions are taking place that could allow cycle access through Wicken Fen as part of the Sustrans National Cycle Network. If successful, this may allow a similar circuit without the need to use the A and B road, so keep an eye out for developments.

From the visitor centre return to the A road and **turn L** to leave Wicken and after approximately 1½ miles **turn L** on the minor road signed for Upware. This leads through a series of bends into Upware and a sharp left-hand bend straight on here leads to the Five Miles pub and a public slipway onto the River Cam, a recommended diversion if only for the views of the river.

Keep with the road at the sharp

The Dyke's End, Reach

box on the left **turn L**, signed for Burwell, by the village sign, then **immediately R** in front of the Dyke's End public house, continuing now on the other side of the green to bear left on Burwell Road, following National Cycle Network Route 51.

The road now winds along slightly higher ground to a junction where **turn L**, signed for National Cycle Network Route 51, on Weirs Drove. Pass a caravan and camping site on the left and newly-planted trees of the Woodland Trust on the right. Continue alongside the pleasant dyke edge, passing an electricity substation on the left, and **turn R** over a bridge, again signed for Route 51, where the road ahead terminates at a gate.

At the T-junction in the village **turn L** by the shops and continue, passing the Anchor on the left. Keep with the road where it is marked as a 'no through road' and on leaving the village, just before the de-restricted speed sign, **turn R** onto the public byway with a small sign for Baulk Farm. A rough earth track then leads between open fields and farm buildings, potholed and with some water and mud in winter, to the B1102 where **turn L**.

left-hand bend, passing sluice gates and boat moorings. Just beyond the buildings of the pump house on the flood bank above to the right, an information board explains about the habitat in the washland between the flood bank and the river.

After a sharp left bend, keep right with the road at a junction on a sharp right bend. The road then proceeds through further bends before a long straight leads to a junction, where you continue more or less straight on to the road marked 'single track road with passing places' and NOT on the road more to the right signed for Swaffham Prior. This leads into Reach after approximately 1½ miles via a sharp left bend after some barns. Keep with the road through the village and shortly after passing the phone

Follow the B road with care as it carries fast traffic and, after passing Ness Farm on the left and just before a level crossing, **turn L** onto the minor Cockpen Road to cross a further level crossing. A steep ramp

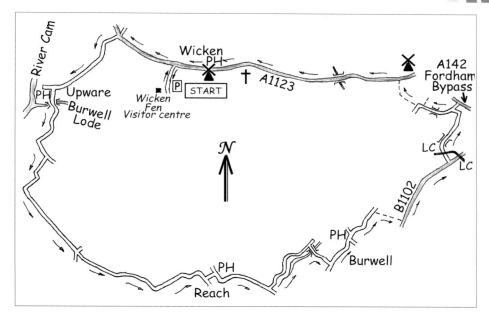

then leads to a bridge over New River after which **turn L** on another minor road near its junction with the new Fordham bypass. Continue over a further bridge and by Lark Hall Farm. Note that at the time of writing the Fordham bypass and changes to the junction of Cockpen and Lark Hall roads are under construction – the description in this guide is based on published plans and discussion with the Council.

After Lark Hall Farm, pass one byway to the right and where the road bends to the left, follow a further byway straight ahead. This leads to the A1123 where **turn L**, to return to Wicken on the higher ground at the fen edge, with occasional glimpses of Ely Cathedral to the right and back to Down Field Windmill in Soham. In Wicken pass the church and windmill on the left and the Maid's Head pub on the right; then **turn L** to return to the visitor centre and parking.

WICKEN FEN

England's oldest nature reserve, famed for its wildlife and one of the last remnants of undrained fenland. This very attractive reserve also houses the last surviving wind water pump, which was relocated from Adventurers' Fen. The National Trust own and operate the reserve, providing nature trails, bird hides, a visitor centre, shop, tearoom and toilets. Admission is free for National Trust members and the fen is open from dawn to dusk every day, with the visitor centre open 10 am to 5 pm from Tuesday to Sunday.

The windpump at Wicken Fen

RECHE (REACH)

A busy port from the 14th to the 18th century, in medieval times it served as the main port for Cambridge. The last recorded load brought here was clunch, a chalky building material used locally until the 1930s. Nowadays it is principally a farming community and a very popular place to live.

THE DYKE'S END PUB, REACH

The Dyke's End was under threat of closure in 1999 as its brewery owners wished to sell it off to be converted into a house. The villagers were having none of this and formed a consortium with the intention of keeping the pub open as a going concern. The District Council challenged the brewery's plans to close the pub and so refused planning permission. The happy result was that the consortium, with advice from the Council, was able to buy the pub by putting up cash in return for shares and it is now a thriving business with a 100% increase in turnover. As a bonus, the Dyke's End can now boast Prince Charles as one of its customers as he flew in by helicopter to visit the pub in his role as Chairman of the Community Trust – an organisation which helps preserve village communities and their amenities.

Anglesey Abbey and the Swaffhams

12½ miles

Cycleways and quiet roads make for a very pleasant route centred on the impressive National Trust property of Anglesey Abbey, including a visit to the quirky Swaffham Prior, with its distinctive skyline of windmills and churches.

Map: OS Landranger 154 Cambridge and Newmarket (GR 532621).

Starting point: Anglesey Abbey where there is free parking. This is just north of the B1102. There is alternative parking in Swaffham Bulbeck if you are not visiting the abbey

By train: Dullingham station (Cambridge–Ipswich line), from where the route can be joined in approximately 3 miles, at the point where the off-road track runs alongside the A14. This is mostly on minor roads, but does involve following a very short section of the A1304, and then crossing the A1303, both of which require care.

Refreshments: There are pubs in Stow cum Quy, Bottisham and both Swaffham Prior and Bulbeck. There is also a licensed restaurant at Anglesey Abbey, which uses local seasonal produce in its freshly prepared home-cooked food.

The route: This is a relatively short route leaving plenty of time to visit Anglesey Abbey, with its gardens and old mill. It keeps primarily away from traffic, but the road from the abbey to Stow cum Quy can be quite busy and has no cycleway, but is soon passed.

From the abbey parking, return to the road and **turn R** to follow the B1102, **with care**, into Stow cum Quy. Immediately on entering the village **turn L**, signed for the Wilbrahams. Shortly pass a pub on the right, ignoring the minor road to then pass the post office on the left.

At the junction with the A1303 by the Prince Albert, **turn L** to join the cycleway and continue alongside the road to the next junction where **turn L**, signed for Bottisham and Swaffham Bulbeck. Follow now either the road or shared-use cycle path to the left into Bottisham and at a junction by the Bell public house **turn L** and then **immediately R**, signed for National Cycle Network Route

The mill at Anglesey Abbey

51 towards Swaffham Bulbeck.

Again, follow either the road or cycle path, now on the right, to cross a small bridge on a left-hand bend and so into Swaffham Bulbeck where the cycle track ends. Pass the church on the left and then just past the phone box **turn R**, signed for Newmarket Road, on Quarry Lane.

After the road bends to the left at the top of a short climb and by a factory, **turn R**, signed for Newmarket. Note, to the left, the skyline of Swaffham Prior, with its two windmills, water tower and two church towers, and follow the road as it undulates before descending towards a bridge over the A14. Do not cross the bridge

but just before it **turn L** onto a minor lane by cottages. Continue straight ahead, almost to the edge of the A14, hidden behind a hedgerow, where **turn L** to follow a byway that runs alongside the A14 between two high hedges.

After approximately 1 mile the byway passes the end of a road where **turn L** and pass Vicarage and Sterling farms, now heading towards Swaffham Prior, noting once again the towers on the skyline.

At the junction with the B1102 road **take care** and cross to the minor road, Cage Hill, directly opposite. Descend slightly into the village and at a T-junction by the village sign, which depicts the distinctive skyline, **turn L**. Continue through the village, now once more on National Cycle Network Route 51, heading for Swaffham Bulbeck, passing the Red Lion public house on the left and then the two churches side by side.

On leaving the village, and as the road approaches the B1102, join the newly-constructed cycle track to the right. which then follows the north side of the B road into Swaffham Bulbeck. Rejoin the road at the end of the cycleway and keep right by the village green and the Black Horse. The cycleway is now once more available adjacent to the road which continues to Lode, where you go straight ahead to return to Anglesey Abbey.

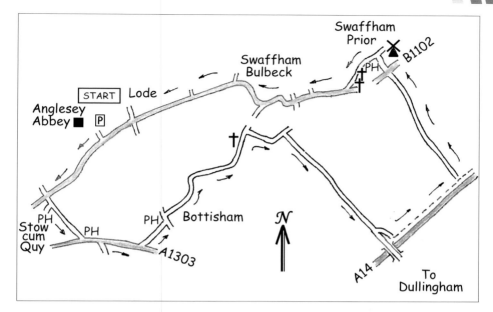

ANGLESEY ABBEY GARDENS AND LODE MILL

Both are well worth a visit, and milling days are on the first and third Saturday of each month. This National Trust Jacobean-style country house is built on the site of a 12th-century Augustinian priory and houses one of the Trust's largest collection of clocks, amongst other things. The formal and informal gardens provide all-year-round interest and some of the plants grown here may be bought at the plant centre. There is also a gift shop, a picnic area and toilets. The house is open from late March to early November and the gardens throughout the year except Christmas week. Cycle parking is available by the entrance and by the staff parking area.

The National Trust and the Royal Society for the Protection of Birds in the East of England have joined forces with the Countryside Agency to form the 'Widen the Choice' Rural Transport Partnership. The aim of this alliance is to encourage more people to visit NT and RSPB sites by bike, thus reducing the pollution and congestion caused by the many car visitors, and adding the health benefits of a bike ride to the enjoyment of a visit to the chosen site. Several of the sites of interest are positioned close to the National Cycle Network or regional cycle routes, and have provided modern cycle parking. Anglesey Abbey is a site that welcomes cyclists and even offers reduced price admission to those arriving by bike!

STOW CUM QUY

Originally two settlements – Stow meaning 'holy place' and Quy 'cow isle' – this is now known locally as Quy.

SWAFFHAM PRIOR

The village is famous for having two churches in one churchyard. St Mary's with its octagonal tower is still in use. St Cyriac's was built a century later for a separate parish and is now used as a social centre. The two windmills, one

Inside the mill at Anglesey Abbey

preserved and one derelict, seem to echo the two churches.

NATIONAL CYCLE NETWORK ROUTE 51

The stretches of Route 51 that feature on this ride are part of the 5,000 miles of cycle network routes now open across the UK courtesy of the vision and hard work of Sustrans. Standing for 'Sustainable transport', the organisation can be traced back to 1977 when a group in Bristol started building cycle routes in an effort to address the dangers to the environment highlighted by the oil crisis. One third of the network has been built on disused railway tracks, forest paths and riversides, with the remaining two-thirds on quiet lanes and traffic-calmed streets. The continuing work of Sustrans involves attempting to find alternative cycling and walking routes to schools, shops and workplaces, in order to reduce damage to the environment by lessening the need for car usage.

Hills and Winding Lanes above the Granta Valley

15½ miles
(plus 4 miles for the detour to visit Chilford Hall Vineyard)

Excellent cycling among some of the highest hills to be found in Cambridgeshire, passing among fields and wooded hilltops that have been moulded through many centuries of occupation and agriculture. This is a very ancient landscape, but there is also the opportunity to visit more recent highlights including an English vineyard and art centre at Chilford Hall.

Map: OS Landranger 154 Cambridge and Newmarket (GR 585507).

Starting point: Balsham, where there is parking near the post office and adjacent to the green. The village is on the B1052, which runs northwards from the A1307 towards Newmarket.

By train: There is no suitable rail start for this route.

Refreshments: On the route there are pubs and shops in Linton, perhaps a little early on the ride, but then there is nothing until the Old Red Lion in Horseheath, a traditional 18th-century inn with modern lodge-style accommodation. Open all day, it is family friendly and has an outdoor seating area. There is also a café at Chilford Hall, and a shop and pub in Balsham.

The route: Although not particularly long, the hills make this a relatively strenuous ride, especially if you decide to detour to the vineyard. The roads used are generally quiet though care is needed through Linton and at the two crossings of the A1307.

From the parking by the post office, head out of the village towards Linton. Pass the green and memorial shelter by a minor road leading to the church on the right. At a junction on the edge of the village, a left turn signed for Linton leads to Chilford Hall Vineyard, an out and back diversion of approximately 4 miles which also involves some descent and so a climb on the return. As an alternative you may wish to visit by car after completing the ride.

If not visiting the vineyard, ignore the left for Linton and take the **next left** for Hildersham and

The round tower church of St Mary's, Bartlow

Abington, with good views ahead and to the left of the area for the day's ride. Cross a public byway, which is the line of an old Roman road, noting the water tower on the hilltop away to the left. Continue to descend, passing farm buildings, and then make a short climb to a crossroads where **turn L**, signed for Linton.

The road bends and undulates just above the valley bottom of the River Granta, leading to Linton where take the **second right**, signed with a weight limit of 7½ tons, onto Symonds Lane. Follow the road through residential streets, taking care when passing parked cars and, at the junction at the bottom of the lane, **turn L**, with shops and a pub to the right.

Continue through the village, passing more pubs and shops, and taking care of the hazard caused by parked cars. At a junction signed for Bartlow, **turn R** and, at the next junction with the busy A1307, **turn R** and then **immediately L**, signed for Bartlow and The Camps. There is a footpath crossing to the right if necessary.

In Bartlow keep straight ahead with the main road at the crossroads and then climb, passing the interesting round-towered church on the right.

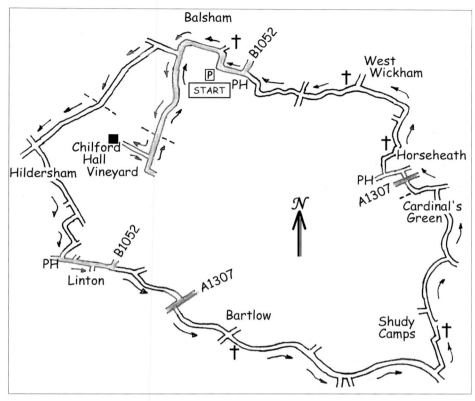

Shortly the road levels out, winding through fields and woodland and passing a cutting through a dismantled railway. Go straight on at the next junction, the road continuing to follow the contour of the land.

Ignore right turns for Ashton and Camps End and climb gradually to a further junction where **turn L**, signed for Shudy Camps and Haverhill. A series of bends then leads into Shudy Camps on the hilltop. Keep straight on through the village, ignoring right and left turns, to descend and then climb once

more to a T-junction by a water tower where **turn L**, signed for Mill Green and Horseheath, now at a height of 375 feet.

The road leads along the hilltop and to Cardinal's Green where, at a junction on a right-hand bend, **turn L** on a more minor road. Keep right with the road at the next junction where a bridleway goes straight ahead and arrive at a 'give way' with the busy A1307. Dismount here and cross to an access point just behind the road sign opposite that leads to a ramp down to a minor lane.

Balsham memorial shelter

Remount and follow the lane to a T-junction in Horseheath where **turn L** and then just past the village hall, by the village sign and with the pub just ahead, **turn R**, signed for West Wickham.

Pass the post office on the right and then the church on the left to climb gradually away from the village, keeping right at the next junction and along the road through Streetly End, with glimpses of the old windmill to the left. In West Wickham go straight ahead with the road, passing the church on the right, to emerge among open fields. The road then winds across the valley, with a further windmill visible to the right in the distance, to a junction in the valley bottom where go straight ahead.

Climb then, with an intermediate descent, into Balsham and at a junction by the Bell public house, **turn L** to return to the parking.

● ●

BALSHAM MEMORIAL SHELTER
Full details of this shelter, which was erected in 1932, and other interesting aspects of the village are explained on the information board on the green opposite.

CHILFORD HALL VINEYARD AND WINERY
The complete wine-making process for the six vine varieties grown here takes place at Chilford Hall Winery. Tours are available at set times from 1st March until 30th October when the vineyard is open from 11 am until 5.30 pm. There is also a café and shop where wine can be sampled and bought.

ST MARY'S CHURCH, BARTLOW
Round-towered churches like this one are very rare in Britain, apart from in Norfolk and Suffolk. There are around 200 examples in these two counties.

THE CAMPS
Shudy Camps and Castle Camps probably share the same name origin. One theory, according to the parish magazine of 1929, is that it derives from Galfridus de Suthecamps who settled this area from Normandy around AD 1200. Nearby Castle Camps owes part of its name to ancient earthworks and a Norman castle.

Studs and Stables along the Suffolk Border

21 miles

A hilly route on quiet lanes through less populous villages that are well away from the influence of the Cambridge suburbs. Newmarket with its horse racing connections is nearby, however, and horses and their related facilities are much in evidence.

Map: OS Landranger 154 Cambridge and Newmarket (GR 618586).

Starting point: Dullingham station, where there is also car parking available. The station is just west of Dullingham village, which is on the B1061 south of Newmarket.

By train: Dullingham, which is on the Cambridge–Ipswich line.

Refreshments: There are not many opportunities to buy refreshments on this route, especially in its first half. If a pub stop is to be made, however, the Red Lion in Kirtling is highly recommended. It offers good drink and food, an outside eating area and is very cyclist friendly. There are also pubs in Brinkley, Saxon Street, Woodditton and Dullingham itself.

The route: The length and frequent climbs make this one of the more strenuous outings in the book. The roads used are generally quiet with only a very small section of B road involved. This means that facilities en route are limited and infrequent, so ensure you set out with a good supply of water.

Turn R out of the car park by the station and after a little way at a staggered junction **turn R**, signed for Westley Waterless and Brinkley, on Balsam Lane. In just over a mile go straight across at a crossroads, and at the next crossroads **turn L**, signed for Brinkley and Haverhill.

Follow the road into Brinkley, joining the B1052, and where the B road bends sharp right, **turn L** onto High Street, heading for Carlton and Great Bradley. Pass the church on the left and continue out of the village. Ignore a left turn for Great Bradley and a right turn for Willingham Green to arrive in Carlton, and at a junction on a right-hand bend **turn L**, signed for Great Bradley, and descend out of the village.

The Rutland Stud

The single-track road leads by a farm, and may be muddy and gravel strewn. Then arriving at a junction with the B1061 **turn R**, still heading for Great Bradley.

In Great Bradley ignore the left turn onto Water Lane and take the **next L** on Hall Road, signed for Cowlinge. Pass the hall and church on the right, cross over the River Stour and then continue through a series of bends to climb away from the valley bottom, ignoring a left turn to East Green. At a crossroads **turn L**, signed for Kirtling and Newmarket.

Another winding road then leads between fields and hedgerows and by farms and cottages to a junction where **turn L**, signed for Kirtling, on Moulting End. Keep right with the road at a junction in Kirtling, passing the Red Lion pub on the left. Descend now, passing the cricket ground, playing field and village hall before arriving at a junction where **turn R** and then **immediately L** by the war memorial, heading for Upend.

A roller coaster road with good views to the right leads into Upend with its pretty thatched cottages. It then climbs, passing Fittocks Stud, and out of the village. Continue, passing further stud farms, to a junction where **turn L** for Cheveley and into Broad Green.

Ignoring right-hand turns for Cheveley and passing a duck pond on the left, the road leads into Saxon Street and to a 'give way' by the village sign opposite the

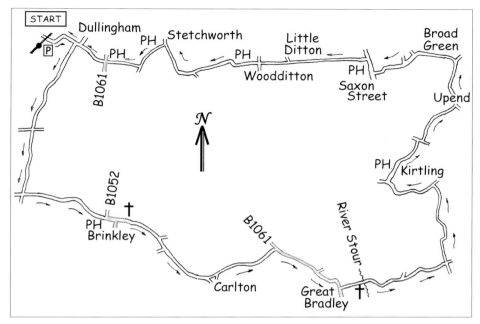

Rutland Stud where **turn R**. Pass the Reindeer pub on the left and then **turn L** for Woodditton on School Road. This leads out of the village accompanied by a shared-use cycle path on the right, if required, to Little Ditton, where the cycle path ends, and then on to Woodditton.

Continue straight on at the crossroads, passing the Three Blackbirds pub and, after a series of bends, a modern water tower on the right just before leaving the village. Keep with the road at the next minor junction, and on into Stetchworth. Pass the Community Centre on the right and then, by the Marquis of Granby pub, **turn L**, signed for Dullingham, which is quickly reached. Keep with the

road to the right at the bottom of the hill, still signed for Dullingham even though we have already passed the village sign.

At the junction with the B1061 by the King's Head, stop and then continue straight ahead on Station Road, signed for Dullingham station, keeping straight on at the next junction to return to our starting point.

• •

RIVER STOUR
The young river, which our route crosses between Brinkley and Carlton, and again in Great Bradley, rises in hills around Brinkley before making its journey to the North Sea on the Suffolk coast, forming the boundary between Essex and Suffolk for much of the way. These hills are a watershed and, to the north-west of

91

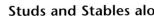

Dullingham station and level crossing

Brinkley, streams drain to the Cam and Ouse and so to the North Sea via The Wash, taking a slightly more circuitous route.

UPEND
Along with its adjoining hamlet of Kirtling, Upend, which is now a conservation village, is described on the structural plan of Cambridgeshire as 'an area of outstanding beauty'.

NEWMARKET
Described as the home of racing, Newmarket began its association with the sport in 1603. Nowadays in the town there are special traffic lights for the horses! The local economy benefits

greatly as the 2,500 racehorses need stabling and training and over 60 stud farms have grown up in the surrounding area, several of which are passed on our route.

SAXON STREET
At one time referred to as 'a considerable hamlet of Woodditton'. Nowadays, though independent and well maintained, Saxon Street is still a part of Woodditton parish. In addition to its beautifully restored and improved residential properties, several large studs (including the Darley and Rutland studs) emphasise the close relationship with Newmarket.

The Cambridgeshire/Norfolk border from Brandon Creek

18½ miles

Starting out from the busy A10 this route very quickly finds peace and solitude, first along the banks of the Little Ouse River and then among tracks and lanes, crossing seldom-frequented fens. The spell is broken briefly for a visit to the busy RAF village of Feltwell, before once more returning to quiet fens and back to the river.

Map: OS Landranger 143 Ely and Wisbech (GR 608919).

Starting point: Brandon Creek, on the A10 north of Ely. There is parking alongside the minor road leading to Bank Farm. Alternative parking is available by the Ship Inn on the other side of the A10.

By train: Lakenheath station on the Ely to Thetford line, from where the route can be joined near Feltwell in approximately 3 miles.

Refreshments: There are few facilities on this ride but if a pub stop is desired the West End pub in Feltwell is recommended. It is open all day, has a beer garden and serves food. On your return to Brandon Creek there is the Ship Inn, normally open lunchtimes and evenings.

The route: There are no hills on this ride but the rough riding along the riverbank on the way out and back make this quite a tiring route, especially if there is a head wind across the fen. The solitude, though, is more than ample compensation, and the off-road sections should be good all year round, though finding and keeping to the right of way along the Little Ouse can be challenging in places.

Follow the minor road from Brandon Creek below the riverbank until reaching Bank Farm. Here take the grassy bridleway to the right and onto the riverbank. After the farm buildings the bridleway drops again from the bank and continues behind a couple of houses at the base of their gardens, then continuing along the field edge below the riverbank. This can be quite heavy going, and following the riverbank itself may be easier. Although this is not the official line of the right of way, certainly, in summer, overgrowth is

Along the bank of the Little Ouse

likely to force you onto the bank at some point.

In Little Ouse where a bridge to the right leads to the church, which has been converted to a domestic dwelling with no public access, continue straight ahead. Where the road shortly turns to the left, again continue straight ahead now on a potholed track below the riverbank, which is a public bridleway. Where the track turns into the last house along the lane, continue straight ahead on an overgrown grassy bridleway, still keeping just below the riverbank. After passing the house the bridleway continues on a clear line just below the bank. The

OS map, however, shows the line of the right of way as being on the bank – so take your choice!

After approximately 500 yards another rough bridleway joins from the left and a grassy ramp gives access to the bank top, and an easy way to switch tracks should you wish. The bridleway then continues on a clear line both on the bank and below to arrive at a substantial agricultural bridge. Join the farm road here, officially by following the rough track to the left or perhaps more conveniently by passing under the bridge.

Keep with the road where it bends

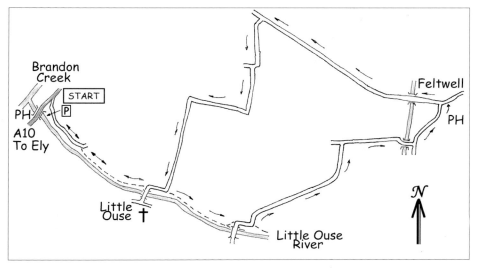

to the left, now heading away from the river on a concrete surface through cropped fields and turf growing operations. This private road, which is also a public bridleway, leads in approximately 2½ miles to a T-junction where **turn R**.

This good road leads in 1½ miles to a further junction where **turn L**, now on a public road and following National Cycle Network Route 30. At the next junction a right turn, signed for National Cycle Network Route 30 and Feltwell, leads through RAF Feltwell to the West End pub, or **turn L** to continue the route.

After leaving Feltwell, cross over the watercourse, and then through a right bend followed by a long straight. In approximately 2 miles **turn L** by Poppylot Farm, signed for Feltwell Anchor. At the next

junction by a barn keep left with the road, still signed for Feltwell Anchor. Keep right at the next junction with a bridleway, again signed for Feltwell Anchor. Shortly the road bends sharp left and then continues in a straight line, leading in 2 miles to the junction in Little Ouse visited earlier. **Turn R** and retrace your steps along the north bank of Little Ouse to Brandon Creek and the parking.

● ●

TURF FARMING

As well as more traditional agriculture this part of the Fens also supports a large amount of turf farming. It is here that much of the lush and verdant cover of many a town garden starts life. Grown from seed in the well-prepared, peat rich, fen soils, the grass quickly forms a dense turf. This is then cut by machines, which produce the now familiar rolls of turf complete with a thin slice of fenland peat, and the process is then repeated.

Mooring at Brandon Creek

THE GREAT AND LITTLE OUSE

Two of the Fens' main rivers meet at Brandon Creek. Both are navigable and while little used for commercial transport these days they remain very popular for recreational cruising. The stretch of the Little Ouse followed by this route is also the boundary between Norfolk and Cambridgeshire.

RAF FELTWELL

The main objective here was originally flying training. During the years 1937 to 1946, squadrons of Bomber Command were stationed on the site. In 1959 Feltwell gained in importance by having the first British Thor IRBM (intermediate range ballistic missile) squadron to reach operational status. Nowadays the RAF station, much in evidence in the town of Feltwell, once again is principally involved in flying training.